the
groom's
speech & duties

hamlyn

confetti.co.uk

First published in Great Britain in 2007 by
Hamlyn, a division of Octopus Publishing Group Ltd
2–4 Heron Quays, London E14 4JP

ISBN-13: 978-0-600-61642-9
ISBN-10: 0-600-61642-8

A CIP catalogue record for this book is available from
the British Library

Printed and bound in China

10 9 8 7 6 5 4 3 2 1

contents

Introduction

Your wedding is, without a doubt, one of the biggest events in your life and you want it to be an occasion to remember for you and your wife, as well as all your family and friends. While the day itself will go by in a whirlwind of excitement, it is a culmination of months of decision-making, careful planning, anticipation and, of course, spending!

Having plucked up the courage to pop the big question, you may well think that you can sit back and relax for a while. Well, think again! As soon as you make your announcement, family and friends will be asking if you've set a date so it's time to start making plans about the kind of day you'd like to have.

The build-up to a wedding is a very exciting time, but it can also be a little daunting. With so much to organize, and ideas and advice coming in from every direction, the groom can often feel overwhelmed. However, while decisions about bridesmaids' dresses, table settings and flowers may well pass you by, you do have a number of important responsibilities.

Although the thought of wading your way through a list of tasks might fill you with dread, the earlier you start, the more relaxed you will be when the big day finally arrives. It's really just a case of good planning and that's why this guide will prove invaluable as you get to grips with your role. It will help you become more informed, more organized and – hopefully – less stressed!

From popping the question to popping the corks for the wedding toast, this book should be your constant companion in the months leading up to your wedding. Packed full of useful information, it will take you through everything you need to know about getting married, offering plenty of helpful tips and advice along the way.

The first chapter talks about the engagement. You may have thought your duties ended as you slipped the ring on to her finger, but what about newspaper announcements, introducing the parents and planning a great engagement party?

The next chapter deals with the wedding itself, covering topics such as marrying abroad, all-important wedding etiquette and even how to tie a Windsor knot.

In the final chapters you will be guided through the part of the wedding that many grooms dread – the groom's speech. Here you'll discover exactly what you should include in your speech, how to get over any nerves you may have and, perhaps most importantly, speech taboos. There is a great selection of sample speeches, jokes, phrases and witty one-liners, all of which will help you write and deliver a speech that's memorable for all the right reasons!

For more ideas and resources, why not visit our website (www.confetti.co.uk). There you will find expert advice on your duties as groom and inspiring ideas for your speech.

The
engagement

The proposal

How to propose

There are a million different ways to propose – on the radio, in the bath, at work, up the Eiffel Tower or floating in a hot-air balloon over the Serengeti sipping champagne. Whatever your chosen approach, the key things to remember are that you should do it for the right reasons and the more romantic the better (although try not to embarrass her). Just remember 'KISS' – Keep it Simple and Sincere!

Should you propose with a ring?

It's up to you. Historically, the man would get down on bended knee and whip out a few rocks on a band of gold. Nowadays, the couple is likely to choose the ring together, and a ring pull from a can often makes do at the crucial moment! You may feel that a proposal isn't a proposal without a ring to hand over, in which case you need to get out there and buy one.

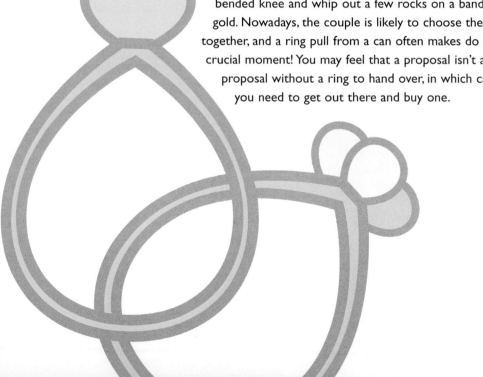

Working out the size of your girlfriend's third finger
If you don't know the size of your girlfriend's ring finger,
you will have to try and find out. Why not ask one of her
best friends to entice her to try on one of her rings for
size and comment on the fit. Alternatively, if she's a deep
sleeper, wind a length of string once around her ring finger
and mark the string with a pen to determine the size. Or
you could 'borrow' a ring that you know she wears on her
ring finger and sneak off to the jewellers with it.
Don't forget that if you do buy a ring ahead
of time and it's not the perfect fit, you
can always have it altered.

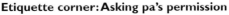

Etiquette corner: Asking pa's permission
Help! I'm planning to propose to my girlfriend soon,
but her father and I don't see eye-to-eye at all. Do
I have to follow tradition and ask him for his
daughter's hand in marriage?

No, you don't, but it might be a good idea if you
do. If you're going to become a part of her family, it's
worth starting off married (or engaged) life on the
right footing with her folks. Her dad has, presumably,
helped bring her up and has been part of moulding
her into the amazingly wonderful person she now is.
You owe it to him to prove that you deserve her,
and it would be great to swallow your pride and
humbly ask for his consent. Your girlfriend will be
more thrilled than anyone. You could always
approach your girlfriend's father after you've
asked her, of course.

Choosing the ring

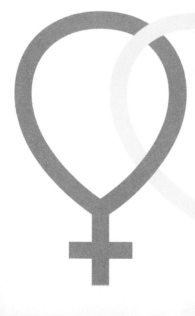

Most engagements are secured with the help of a big sparkler. Traditionally, it is up to the man to pay for the ring, and one popular guideline (admittedly perpetrated by the diamond industry) is that it should cost two months' salary. It should be left to you to decide whether that's net or gross!

It's best to steer clear of second-hand rings, unless they are quality antiques or family heirlooms, and even then be careful. If you are thinking about giving your girlfriend a family heirloom, make sure that it is to her taste and will fit her ring finger or can be altered to fit.

You should always keep the receipt for the ring, just in case she hates the one you have chosen, turns you down or if you ever need to make an insurance claim. Make sure the ring is insured as soon as possible. If you are planning to pop the question abroad, check that the ring is covered by your travel insurance, in case it drops from your pocket en route to that tropical desert island.

Note, if your fiancée calls off the engagement, the ring should be returned to you. If you call it off, she gets to keep it, and it's up to her what she does with it.

Ring-buying tips

Make sure that the engagement ring and wedding ring will go well together when worn. Wedding rings are usually made from gold, white gold, red gold or platinum. The engagement ring generally looks more stylish if it is made from the same metal as the wedding ring.

- Have the ring size measured properly (in any jewellers). The ring should not fit too tightly or it may get stuck and she won't be able to get it on or off. Equally, the ring should not be so loose that it slides around on her finger or over her knuckle too easily.

- There are thousands of styles of engagement ring to choose from, and it's worth taking time to find the right one – after all, your fiancée will be wearing it for a lifetime. Shop around and make sure you buy from a reputable company.

Announcing your engagement

It's usually best to tell close family the news of your engagement first before spreading the news far and wide. How you do this is up to you – you can do it by phone, e-mail, in person or even over the tannoy at the supermarket.

To let everyone else know, wedding announcements are traditionally placed in the local and national newspapers by the bride's parents. But you can place announcements yourself, or follow the modern route that is becoming popular and announce it online, using an Internet service such as www.confetti.co.uk.

Setting the date

You may have a specific date in mind, or you may be quite open. Either way, it's worth bearing in mind that it's often easier to find available dates for venues, registrars etc. outside the traditional wedding season (May to September).

Try and be as sensitive as possible when setting the date. For instance, picking the week before the bride's sister is due to get married could cause some serious family upset. Remember, don't announce the date, print invitations or make arrangements until you have received written commitment from the venue as well as the celebrant.

Planning a wedding takes a fair amount of time and effort, so unless you are going for a really simple event or have lots of help available, leave yourself a reasonable period of time between getting engaged and married. The average engagement nowadays lasts 19 months.

Etiquette corner: Parental introductions

Isn't there a rule that the groom's parents should introduce themselves to the bride's parents after the engagement has been announced?

It is traditional for the groom's parents to 'call on' the bride's parents soon after their offspring have decided to marry, but it doesn't always happen these days. Generally, the parents will meet at some stage during the engagement (it would, after all, be a mite strange for them to meet at the wedding), but engagements now are longer and there doesn't seem to be any hurry to make the Introductions. It's a nice idea, though, to arrange a get-together as soon as possible after the engagement.

The cost of a wedding

Working out your budget

There's only one real rule when it comes to budgeting for your wedding: plan for the type of wedding you can realistically afford.

How much will it cost?

The average wedding costs somewhere in the region of £14,000. Around £1,200 of that is spent on the rings, £1,400 on the wedding outfits and essential pampering in the run-up to the big day, and £1,300 on the wedding itself. The reception costs around £3,500 and, finally, of course, there's the honeymoon and other expenses that vary from couple to couple.

Opening a wedding account

Paying for your wedding using a credit card is likely to lead to nuptial nightmares. It's not unheard of for a couple to spend so much on their cards that they are divorced before they have paid for their wedding! Instead, open a designated wedding account and start paying in a regular sum each month, preferably by standing order or direct debit. All bills can be paid from this account and it's easy to keep track of how much is being spent, as well as keeping a check on deposits paid to the venue and so on.

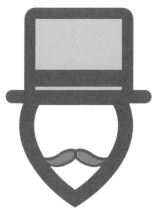

Who pays for what?

Traditionally, it falls to the father of the bride to pick up the tab for the main event, with the groom paying for the church or register office fees and the all-important honeymoon. But more and more couples now choose to pay for the bulk of their wedding themselves. It's important to work out from the start who is paying for what and whether there are any financial constraints. For example, is the bride's father willing to pay for the horse and carriage to the church? And how many guests can you afford to invite to the main reception?

The best advice is to use the list below as a kick-off point and discuss who will do (and pay for) what as soon as you and your fiancée have set a date for your wedding.

Paying for the wedding
Bride's family
Traditionally, the bride's family pays for:

- engagement and wedding press announcements
- the bride's and bridesmaids' dresses (many brides now pay for their own dress)
- outfits for the mother and father of the bride
- flowers for the church and reception (the groom pays for the bouquets and buttonholes)
- photographer/videomaker
- most of the transport
- wedding stationery
- the reception and all that entails – the big expense!

Groom

Traditionally, the groom pays for:

- the wedding rings
- the hire and cost of his own clothes
- all church/register office expenses
- the bride's bouquet
- the bridesmaids' flowers
- buttonholes for the male members of the wedding party
- transport
- presents for the best man, ushers and bridesmaids
- the hotel on the first night
- the honeymoon

Etiquette corner: The groom's family's contribution

Can my parents contribute to the cost of the wedding?

Often the groom's parents are pleased to contribute financially to the occasion in some way, but this is not a foregone conclusion. If your parents make an offer and you are happy for them to contribute, then make a list of who's paying for what as soon as possible, to avoid any misunderstandings. One common solution is for the groom's family to provide the wedding cake and pay for any food at the evening reception. Or you may want to do a straight 50:50 split. Tread carefully, though. Ask them first what they have in mind.

Budgeting for the wedding

Sticking to your budget

It's essential to set a limit on the amount you spend, whoever is paying. Planning your wedding is stressful enough without arguments erupting over the costs. Add a further ten per cent to your budget to cope with the inevitable extras. For an interactive budget planner, check out: www.confetti.co.uk

Taking out insurance

Wedding insurance is well worth considering. It will cover you for a number of eventualities, such as damage to the bride's dress, theft of presents, cancellation of the reception (because of illness of a parent, for example) and double booking of the venue. Bear in mind, though, that wedding insurance won't cover you if either of you get cold feet on the big day!

Tips for saving money

- Think about what you actually want at your wedding, and what you think you could do without (for instance, do you need a video as well as photographs?).
- The easiest way to save money is not to pay over the odds. So shop around for the venue, caterers, photographer and so on. Ask for quotations in writing and make sure you know exactly what the price agreed covers. Remember that you may need to add VAT to some prices, so always ask.
- Consider a weekday wedding, when venues generally charge quite a lot less.

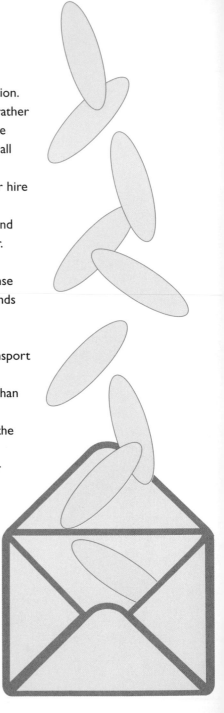

- Check if you can supply your own wine for the reception. For your toast, opt for an inexpensive sparkling wine rather than champagne, then have a pay bar for the rest of the evening. If there's no bar at your venue, you could ask all your guests to bring a bottle!
- Hire your suit and the bride's wedding dress or buy or hire a worn-once suit or dress.
- Ask either set of parents to do the church flowers – and save on florist's costs. Seasonal flowers will be cheaper.
- Use a good photographer, but preferably one whose company is small enough not to charge VAT. Or dispense with a photographer altogether and ask your arty friends to take your photos. At the reception, put disposable cameras on each table.
- Make use of friends with posh cars like Jaguars to transport the wedding party to the church or venue.
- Invite more casual friends to an evening drink rather than the full wedding with all its catering costs.
- Ask a relative or friend with culinary talents to make the cake as their wedding gift to you.
- Forego the professional DJ and play your own CDs or tapes or ask an aspiring DJ friend to do their thing.
- You may even decide to ask guests to chip in for your celebration, although for many people this is a contentious issue. Some couples get round this by having an informal reception and asking guests to bring a specific dish or contribute to a buffet.
- Leave for your honeymoon on a weekday. Consider an all-inclusive hotel package.
- Ask your guests to give you honeymoon vouchers as a present.

Your best man

The best man's role is, briefly, to be supportive of the groom in the run-up to the wedding, organize a stag night, marshal the ushers on the day, make sure the rings make it to the church and give the best man's speech. Many grooms split the best man's duties between two friends or relatives: one to take on the pre-wedding duties, including organizing the stag night, and the other to perform the role on the day. Having two best men at the actual wedding can be fun – they could make a joint speech, which would certainly be different!

Can you have a female best man?

If your best mate/best choice for best man is a woman, it's advisable to make sure that you and the bride are in agreement over this one, as it's just possible she might not be keen on another woman at the altar on her big day. If she has no reservations, then go right ahead.

Double the fun

If you can't – or don't want to – decide between two friends, it's fine to have two best men. If both are present, they can stand up front with you during the ceremony, and you can divide up the day's responsibilities as follows:

- One brings the rings, the other acts as toastmaster for the speeches, cake cutting, etc.
- One is master of ceremonies for the day, the other makes the speech.
- They make a joint best-man speech and hand over one ring each.

Choosing your ushers

Being an usher is a nice honour to bestow on your friends or brothers. There's no strict rule as to how many ushers you should have, but as their main role is to organize the guests at the ceremony, a smaller venue will suggest fewer ushers, and a larger one more. As a rule of thumb, you should have a minimum of one usher per 50 guests.

The ushers answer directly to the best man and should be available to help out when and where they can, calmly and politely ironing out any last-minute creases and adding greatly to the smooth running of the day. This could mean assisting a wheelchair-bound guest to their place at the venue, slipping away in advance to light the lanterns for a winter wedding procession or even helping to hand round food or drinks.

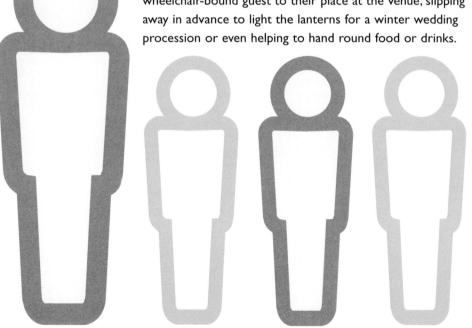

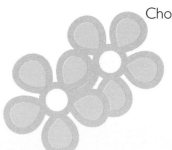

The ushers' responsibilities

- Ushers should dress in the style of the groom and best man. So, if you are in morning dress, they should be, too, although you and your best man may have a flower buttonhole of a different colour from the ushers.
- The ushers should meet at the wedding venue some time before the ceremony begins and well before the arrival of any early guests.
- Ushers should be able to recognize the 'key players' at the wedding, especially the bride and groom's parents. Having ushers from the bride's side and also from the groom's will greatly help here, as well as contributing in a practical way to the symbolic union of two families, which a wedding represents.

- The chief usher should delegate tasks such as giving out service sheets and should also have a seating plan for the front rows (from the best man) and be briefed about any family friction that may need to be negotiated. He should escort the bride's mother – who is the last to take her seat before the entrance of the bridal party – to her seat on her arrival at the church.
- At least one usher should stand at the back during the service, to welcome latecomers and discreetly guide them to any available seat.
- At least one usher should stand at the foot of the aisle to ask guests on which side they are to sit: groom's friends and family on the right, bride's on the left.

- Another usher should position himself halfway down the aisle to guide people to their seats.
- Outside the wedding venue, ushers may be asked to find specific guests for the photographer's pictures, or – more likely – to help organize transport for the guests from the wedding venue to the reception.
- At the reception venue, ushers should direct guests to the room where the bride and groom would like them to assemble and be ready to lend a hand if needed.

The stag party

Although it's the task of your best man to make all the arrangements for the stag night, if you have strong ideas on what you want to do – or definitely don't want to do – let him know firmly and early on. If you're short on ideas try looking on the Internet for inspiration.

Traditionally, the lads treat you to the big bash as well as covering their own costs. It is therefore important to agree beforehand on what kind of stag night everyone can afford to take part in. If you're keen on going somewhere pricey, you might want to let it be known that you will contribute towards the bill.

Remember that holding your stag night right before your wedding is to be avoided – you need to give yourself time to recover!

Joint stag and hen night

Traditionally, stag and hen nights marked a farewell to your same-sex group of friends before the start of married life, and it still heralds a goodbye to the single life. Therefore, most people tend to view them as single-sex events, although, to an extent, this depends entirely on what you want to do – you may be happier having a boozy lad's night out rather than partying with a mixed group. However, couples are increasingly holding combined stag and hen nights. If most of your friends know each other, then this has its advantages, but there are also practical considerations, such as the matter of babysitters if your friends have children.

Great stag nights

Do you want to spend a weekend being active? Being creative or cultural? In the lap of luxury? Or do you want a traditional boozy weekend? Do you want to party close to home, or would a weekend away go down well? Maybe you want to go abroad for a stag weekend to really remember. Whatever you decide, here are some great ideas for group activities.

Top ideas for stag nights

- For daredevils and adrenaline junkies book up for a stag bungee jump, or take to the skies in a stunt plane to loop-the-loop and barrel roll! White-water rafting, trapezing above lakes and rivers on a zip wire or zooming about in a powerboat off the coast are great ideas for summer stags.
- For action men enjoy a day of paintballing where you can team up and practise your SAS skills, or how about dry-slope skiing or snowboarding for a day's action. Alternatively, if the budget's tight, have a game of football or rounders in a local park and follow it up by after-action pints in a favourite pub.
- For party animals, pack your bags and take to the skies for a mad weekend away! The most popular places to head for include Amsterdam, Barcelona and Dublin.
- For gamblers, have a night at the dogs or set up a mini casino at home. Don't just stop at a day at the races, go for the double! Combine Chester and Aintree, Lingfield and Epsom, or Doncaster and York to give yourself twice as many opportunities of winning enough cash to cover all those last-minute wedding expenses. For an ultimate weekend of gambling, fly out to Las Vegas on Friday afternoon. This is a 24-hour city with no 'last orders'!
- For those who like pampering, book into a spa retreat or health farm and enjoy massages and utter relaxation.

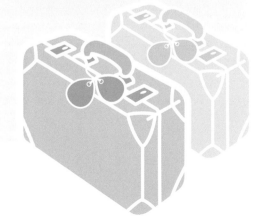

Pre-wedding checklist

By the time your wedding day arrives you should feel confident that everything is organized and everyone knows their responsibilities. Use this checklist as a guide to what you need to do at various stages in the lead-up to your big day.

Six months before the wedding

- Confirm date and booking with the church or register office and the reception venue. Pay deposits or fees, if required at this stage.
- Choose your best man and ushers.
- Choose and book the photographer (and videomaker, if you're having one).
- Choose and book the band or DJ for the reception.
- Choose and order your wedding rings. This will allow plenty of time for fittings and adjustments.
- Finalize guest numbers and write your guestlist.
- Book the honeymoon (see honeymoon checklist on page 61).
- Choose and book your transport for the wedding day.
- Choose and reserve your outfits, as well as those for your best man, ushers and the fathers.
- Choose and order your wedding stationery.
- Organize wedding insurance.

Three months before the wedding

- Organize your marriage licence.
- Have a meeting with the caterer at your reception venue and choose the menu and wine.
- Send out the wedding invitations.

- If you're having a wedding list, decide on where it will be held and make an appointment to choose the gifts.
- Meet with the vicar or registrar to discuss your ceremony requirements, music and readings.

One month before the wedding
- Arrange a suit fitting and try to get everyone there for the same appointment. Remember to take with you the shoes you'll be wearing at the wedding.
- Reconfirm bookings with everyone involved in the wedding.
- Start writing your speech, or making some notes at least.
- Work out the seating plan for the reception.
- Book a hotel room for the wedding night.
- Buy presents for your best man, ushers and bridesmaids.

One week before the wedding
- Book a taxi to take you to your hotel or the airport.
- Collect your suit and try it on again.
- Finalize your speech and rehearse it.
- Ensure your best man and ushers know what to do.

One day before the wedding
- Arrange your clothes, shoes and accessories for the day.
- Have a church wedding rehearsal with the key people.
- Check that you have everything packed if you're going straight to a hotel.
- Give sufficient cash to your best man to pay suppliers on the day and make sure he knows how much is owed.
- Give your rings and a copy of your speech to the best man.
- Check you have a copy of your speech and any messages that need to be read out at the reception.

The
wedding

Where to marry

If you and/or your partner are religious, you may well choose to get married in a church. However, if you have no religious affiliations, or different religious beliefs, you might decide on a civil ceremony. Some of the choices and different types of ceremony are outlined below.

Marrying abroad

The idea of marrying abroad can be very attractive. Just imagine a sandy beach, blue skies and palm trees while you make your vows, or how about the excitement of a 'drive-thru' wedding in Vegas?

How will your family react?

By getting married abroad, you are bound to disappoint some members of your family and friends who cannot join you on the day. To appease any objections, you could have a blessing or reception when you return.

Keeping it private

Be aware that many hotels abroad perform more than one ceremony each day and you could also be the main attraction for hotel guests. Ask your tour operator or hotel for details, but if you want to be certain of a private ceremony, then consider a quiet or unusual destination.

Leaving it to the professionals

The most fuss-free way to organize a wedding abroad is to book with a reputable, bonded travel agent or tour operator specializing in arranging such events.

Wedding packages are available in many hotels. The service is nearly always civil, although religious ceremonies and blessings can be arranged in most destinations. Packages tend to include the basic requirements: service, marriage licence, certificate and legal fees, but these differ between hotels. If you want extras, such as photographs or a cake, then expect to pay more, and remember that any extras may be fairly basic compared to what you might expect at home. Check with your tour operator for details.

You can arrange your own wedding abroad but this will involve researching legal requirements and residency rules plus organizing the details, from the ceremony to the flowers.

Keeping it legal

To be legally married in the UK, these requirements must be fulfilled:

- You must both be at least 16 years old. (In England and Wales, if either party is under 18 written consent must be obtained from parents or legal guardian.)
- You must not be closely related.
- The marriage must take place in premises where marriage can be legally solemnized, including register offices, premises that have a civil licence authority, parish churches of the Church of England and churches that have been registered by the register general for worship and marriage. There are exceptions for military marriages and for those detained or housebound.
- The ceremony must take place in the presence of a Superintendent Registrar, a Registrar or an authorized person.
- In England and Wales, the ceremony must take place between 8am and 6pm (except for the Jewish religion and the Society of Friends). In Scotland you can marry at any time of the day.
- Two people must witness the ceremony.
- You must both be free and eligible to marry.

Ceremony choices
Church weddings

For most people, a church wedding means marrying in the picturesque church in the village where the bride's parents live. However, marrying in a church is all about getting married in the eyes of God. If neither of you has any real religious convictions, it would be respectful to think carefully about why you want a church wedding.

Church of England weddings

A Church of England wedding is both a civil ceremony and a religious one, with religious music and readings. The vicar is legally registered to perform the civil ceremony as well as the religious rites.

If the church is in your parents' or your own parish, your vicar will organize the marriage licence. If not, you can apply for a common licence and need to have a good reason for the vicar as to why you want to get married in that parish.

By law, marriages can take place on any day of the week between 8am and 6pm, but most happen on a Saturday between 10am and 4pm. The vicar will normally discourage weddings during Lent (the 40 days before Easter).

Publishing the banns

The notice of your impending marriage has to be read out in church on three consecutive Sundays before the wedding, and you should attend at least one of the services. If you and the bride are from different parishes, the banns will be read in both. The wedding can take place any time within the next three calendar months after the banns have been read. If this doesn't happen, they will have to be read again.

Guests

If you're getting married in a small church, some friends may have to be invited to the reception only. If it's a large church, make sure you have enough guests to fill it, otherwise there will be little atmosphere.

It's traditional for the bride's family and friends to be seated on the left-hand side of the altar and the groom's on the right-hand side.

Most people opt for formal wear. There is no strict dress code, but the general rule is to dress for the occasion.

Making your vows

Getting married in a church offers you less freedom to write your own vows than if you're tying the knot in a civil ceremony. Usually, the only part you can change is the 'obey' aspect and to opt for 'respect' rather than 'honour'.

Settling the bill

Traditionally, the groom pays for all the church expenses. Either settle the account before the wedding day or let the best man settle it.

Roman Catholic weddings

If you or your intended are Roman Catholic, even non-practising, you will usually be allowed to marry in a Catholic church on condition that you sign up to some basic Catholic principles. If one partner is not a Catholic, you will need to obtain a dispensation for a 'mixed marriage'. The wedding usually takes place in the parish of the bride and/or groom.

The service is a religious one, usually also covering the civil aspect of a wedding, since most priests are empowered to act as Registrars. You may be married with or without a Mass (the full Catholic religious service). Weddings during the season of Lent are not encouraged, although they will not be refused, except for the three days before Easter Sunday. You will have to obtain the marriage licence but the priest will arrange the publishing of the banns.

The Roman Catholic Church's strict rules on marriage mean that it is virtually the only mainstream Christian church that doesn't allow remarriage of divorcées. Exceptions are made if a first marriage was not recognized by the Church. Divorcées, however, can have a blessing.

The standard Catholic marriage ceremony more or less dictates what your vows are.

It's customary to give the priest a donation. How much is up to you and what you can afford – £50–£70 is reasonable.

Unitarian weddings

Unitarianism is a historic non-conformist faith that emphasizes individual choice and deciding for yourself in spiritual matters. Members may come from a variety of religious backgrounds, their beliefs ranging from liberal Christian to religious humanist to New Age.

Unitarians are happy to perform ceremonies for couples of different faiths – for example, Christian and Jewish – and for divorcées. In fact, divorcées actually form a higher percentage of those getting married in Unitarian churches and chapels than for any other denomination or faith.

Blessings

Many couples opt for a civil wedding, but some decide to have a blessing, too. A blessing is a short ceremony that takes place after the official marriage. A blessing is not legally binding, it's a spiritual way of symbolizing commitment.

Blessings are flexible and a great way to inject a religious dimension into an otherwise fairly secular occasion. A formal religious blessing must be performed by a priest, but blessings don't have to be religious.

Why have a blessing?

In the case of inter-denominational or inter-faith couples, it can be tricky to satisfy both religions. One compromise is to be married in one religious tradition and have a blessing in the other. Since Catholics are not allowed to remarry in church, divorcées often opt for a blessing.

Organizing a blessing

There is no time limit on when you can have a blessing. Some couples opt for it to take place on the wedding day, others prefer it a few days after the wedding.

The person you want to give the blessing should be a recognized official of whatever tradition you follow. Explain exactly what you want and discuss how best to go about it.

Ceremony choices
Civil weddings

There are many reasons why you might choose to have a civil wedding: you might have no religious beliefs, it could be your second marriage or perhaps you want to get married somewhere a bit different. Whatever your reason for wanting to tie the knot, no Superintendent Registrar can refuse to marry you, unless there is a legal reason to prevent it.

What is a civil ceremony?
- It contains no religious elements or anything with religious connotations (including music and readings).
- It is conducted and registered by a Superintendent Registrar or Registrar.
- It must take place after 8am and before 6pm, any day of the week, subject to staffing arrangements.
- The Registrar has to receive an 'Authority' for your marriage to be able to proceed, which can be obtained only by giving a Notice of Marriage (see pages 38).

Where can you get married?
The classic alternatives to getting married in a church are in a register office – a local venue that is ordained specifically for performing weddings – or in an approved premises (licensed venues). Most approved premises are hotels.

Approved premises must be permanently moored, have a roof, be open for public use and be approved for use for weddings by the Superintendent Registrar of the district. This means you can't have a civil wedding in

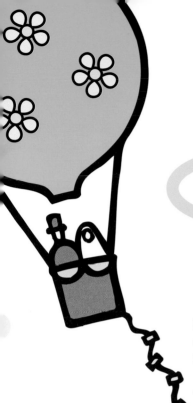

your garden or in a hot air balloon, but you can have a civil ceremony on Brighton Pier or in the clubhouse at Stamford Bridge, both of which have licences.

The more unusual options

If you'd like your wedding to be a little out of the ordinary, look into the following:

- Marrying abroad (see pages 30–31).
- Humanist ceremony. This secular ceremony isn't legally binding but it can take place absolutely anywhere. So you could have a register office ceremony first then hold a humanist ceremony afterwards in your dream location. This can be a particular advantage for couples from different faiths.
- DIY ceremony. More like a party and not legally binding (you must have a register office ceremony first), you can create the celebration of your dreams.

The formalities

You are entitled to marry in a civil ceremony at any register office in the UK or approved premise in England or Wales. You both have to give a Notice of Marriage in person in the district in which you live, even if you both live in the same district, and pay a fee. For this, you may need to produce original documentation such as your birth certificate and passport. Check with the register office for requirements.

A copy of the Notice will then go on display publicly within the register office. Provided there is no legal objection, the Authority for your marriage will then be issued after 15 days, and is valid for a year from the date of your Notice. It is your responsibility to ensure that **both** Notices will be valid for the date of your marriage. Visitors choosing to marry in England or Wales will need to satisfy the residential qualification of seven days and then wait a further 15 clear days before they are eligible to marry.

The practicalities

Note that register offices and civil venues have a maximum number of guests that can be accommodated for safety reasons, and that includes babies and children.

For register office weddings first book the date with the Registrar in the register office you wish to get married in. If you decide to have readings or music in your ceremony, this should be submitted and discussed with the Registrar prior to the service for his or her approval.

For civil venue weddings first select the licensed venue you intend to marry in and check the availability of the Registrar at your local register office. Book them both. Find out from the venue what form the ceremony can take and see above for register office requirements.

Dress

You have the option to be as formal or informal as you like. The bride can wear anything, from a smart outfit or full wedding dress to fancy dress, while you could wear full morning suit or perhaps a lounge suit.

The ceremony

All those attending the ceremony should arrive in the building no later than about five minutes beforehand. In some register offices and most civil venues, it is possible for the bride to make an entrance on someone's arm. Before the ceremony begins, the Registrar will see the bride and groom to check that the information stated on the Authority is correct. Any fees due will also need to be paid at this stage.

Many couples adopt traditional church etiquette, for example having bridesmaids and a best man and setting up an 'aisle'. The only real rule is that nothing with religious connotations can be incorporated into the ceremony.

Ceremony choices
Civil partnerships

Civil Partnerships (CPs) give gay and lesbian couples the same legal rights as a married couple. Previously, only 'commitment ceremonies' existed, and these didn't give gay couples the same rights as a married couple.

The Civil Partnership Act 2004 finally came into force in December 2005, paving the way for thousands of same-sex couples to begin planning for their weddings.

Registration of a civil partnership is different to a civil marriage in that it is not officially recognized as a marriage under UK law. It is, however, very much a celebration of the union of two people who have chosen to devote their lives together, and for that reason it can be called a gay wedding.

Arranging your civil partnership registration

A civil partnership can be formed in England and Wales at a register office or at any other approved venue, including hotels, stately homes and other places of interest.

To form a civil partnership you must first give notice of your intention to become civil partners. This means that you are legally required go to your nearest register office and inform them of your wish to register your civil partnership. Your details are then made public by the registration authority for a period of fifteen days. Your notice is valid for 12 months from that date and you can arrange your ceremony or simply sign the registration schedule anytime during that year.

Legal status

- Registration of a civil partnership differs from a civil marriage in that whilst it is legally binding it is not legally referred to as a marriage.
- Additionally, whilst civil marriages can only be entered into by hetereosexual couples, civil partnerships can only be entered into by same-sex couples.
- Under the new Civil Partnership Act gay couples, or 'civil partners,' will finally be able to enjoy many of the same rights as heterosexual married couples.

The ceremony

As civil partnership registration is a completely secular process, just like the civil marriage ceremony, you are prevented from having any religious service take place at the time of your registration.

A ceremony is not automatically provided when you register. Couples who wish to arrange for a ceremony at the time of registration should discuss this with the registrar when the initial arrangements are made. If you fancy walking down the aisle to the tune of a favourite piece of music you'll need to make sure it has no religious connotations as your ceremony has to be free of any mention of religion.

You will have the opportunity to say some words before you sign the registration schedule and you'll need to bring with you at least two other people as witnesses. If you did want to have a more spiritual ceremony, you could always arrange a separate humanist or other type of ceremony which would have special meaning to you. Couples who marry in civil weddings have the same limitations and often choose to have a humanist wedding ceremony as well as their civil wedding service.

What to wear

Formal attire

Ideally, the principal adult male members of the wedding party (including the bride's father) should all dress alike, although you, as the groom, may choose to be slightly different. To create the perfect coordinated look visit the outfitters with your best man, the ushers and, if possible, your father and the bride's father.

If you are planning to lose a fair amount of weight – or bulk up the muscles to impress your bride on your honeymoon – then remember to factor this in when deciding when to hire or buy your suit.

If hiring, you should book your clothes at least three months before the wedding, allowing time for alterations to be carried out, if necessary. It should be remembered that some weeks of the year will be busier than others and demand will consequently be higher. If your wedding date falls in this period, it may be necessary to book even earlier to avoid disappointment.

The choice of shoes is personal, although the rule is not to wear brown shoes with black trousers and vice versa. A well-fitting pair of leather shoes is your best choice, regardless of how comfortable your old trainers are.

Lounge suit

The important thing at any event, and especially at your wedding, is to feel at ease. If more formal dressing makes you feel uncomfortable, then lounge suits are a good alternative. This is definitely a sharp and sophisticated choice, and while

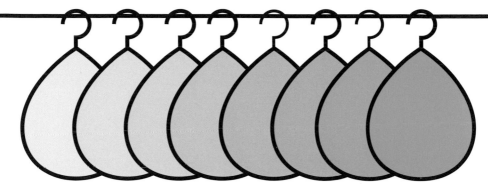

associated with register office weddings, is perfectly acceptable for religious weddings as well.

Should you (or the bride) be keen on creating a coordinated look, you can mix a lounge suit with any shirt and tie, which can easily be matched or contrasted with the wedding colour theme.

Looking good

If you're not quite at your fighting weight or think that you could do with a new hairstyle or look, then what better incentive for getting into shape than looking good on your wedding day.

- Remember to diet and exercise sensibly – you don't want to overdo it and look haggard and grey in the photos.
- It may take two or three cuts to get the hairstyle you want, so see your hairdresser at

least three months before the wedding. Try to resist the temptation to surprise your bride by turning up at the altar having shaved your beard off, grown a moustache or dyed your hair. It could all go horribly wrong.

- If you're prone to five o'clock shadow or you're particularly nervous, then you may want to have a professional shave on the morning of your

wedding. Apart from anything else, it is a wonderfully relaxing experience.

- A manicure a day or two before the big day will leave your nails cleaner than you've ever seen them, which is wise if you're doing the ring thing. Don't be shy – everyone is at it these days!

Dress code

It is not only acceptable but also welcome to guests to have the dress code indicated on the invitation. This may be suggested in a number of ways, such as the succinct 'Black Tie', which essentially means tuxedos for gentlemen, and evening dresses for ladies, or 'White Tie', which means tails for men, and ball- or full-length gowns for women. 'Morning Dress' and 'Lounge Suit' are terms not used very often these days and are best avoided if you don't want calls from anxious or confused guests! However, if you wish your dress code to be something out of the ordinary, you can always say 'Fancy Dress', 'Purple Attire', 'Denim and Diamonds' or whatever takes your fancy!

Morning dress

The morning suit (penguin suit, top hat and tails) is usually worn for weddings before 3pm, and is still the most popular attire. The cut and style of the coat is very flattering to the majority of figures, and consists of a blue, black or grey tailcoat paired with matching or contrasting trousers, either plain or pinstriped. The outfit is completed by a white wing-collar shirt, a waistcoat of any colour, a cravat, a top hat and gloves (just held, not worn).

Black tie

Black tie is traditionally worn for weddings later in the day or for those to be followed by a formal reception, and is ideal for a grand evening reception or summer ball. Obviously, if you're opting for black tie, you should inform your guests of this dress code, too.

You should wear a black dinner jacket, either single- or double-breasted, with ribbed silk lapels and no vents or covered buttons. Trousers should be tapered, suitable for braces and, officially, have one row of braid. The evening shirt, in cotton or silk, with either a Marcella or a pleated front, has a soft, turn-down collar.

The bow tie is of black silk. Cummerbunds may be worn (with pleats opening upwards), but waistcoats are still much more acceptable. Black tie can be made as individual as you like with a colourful bow tie, matching waistcoat and pocket-handkerchief. Shoes should be black and well-polished, and socks plain black.

Got the blues?

Many grooms in the armed forces choose to be married wearing their regimental uniform, which is not only ceremonial but also well suited to the traditions of a wedding. The traditional uniform for weddings is the Blues uniform: a blue jacket with a high collar, adorned with five brass buttons down the front and two on each cuff for officers. The jacket is teamed with matching blue trousers with a red stripe down the outside of each leg. No shirt is worn but the uniform is accessorized with a white belt and gloves. Military uniform may be worn by all grooms who are full-time members of the armed services.

Traditional outfit

The best-known and most popular of these is Highland morning or evening dress, traditionally worn by Scottish grooms. The kilt should be accompanied by a Bonnie Prince Charlie jacket or doublet, a sporran, laced brogues, socks, bow tie, and *sgian-dhu* (a small dagger carried in your sock).

How to tie a tie

The Bow Tie

1 Start with A 4 cm (1½ in) below B.
2 Take A over then under B.
3 Double B in half and place across the collar points.
4 Hold B with thumb and finger; drop A over.
5 Pull A through a little, then double A and pass behind, then through the hole in front.
6 Poke resulting loop through; even it out, then tighten.

The Four-in-Hand

1 Start with A about 50 cm (20 in) below B.
2 Take A behind B.
3 Continue wrapping right round.
4 Pull A up through the loop.
5 Pull A down through loop in front.
6 Tighten.

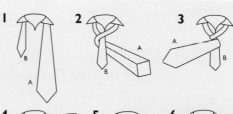
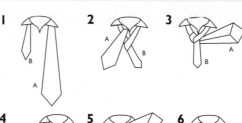

The Windsor

1 Start with A about 60 cm (24 in) below B.
2 Take A behind B and up through loop.
3 Bring A over and behind B.
4 Take A down through loop again.
5 Then over and up through loop.
6 Bring through the knot and tighten.

What happens just before the wedding?

The wedding rehearsal

A rehearsal for a church wedding ceremony usually takes place the evening before the wedding or a few days before the wedding, depending on when the main participants are available. You need wear only casual clothes for this.

A rehearsal is essential, especially for elaborate weddings, so that the main participants know the procedure. The vicar will take everyone through the service and show everyone their positions and where and when to move.

The morning of the wedding

Tradition says that it is bad luck for the bride and groom to see each other on the morning of the wedding, but practicalities may dictate otherwise.

If the bride is getting ready at her parents' home and the groom at a local hotel or friend's house, this is an easy tradition to follow. But if the couple live together, are getting married abroad or are far away from home, it may be necessary for them to see each other on the morning of the wedding. If one or both of you is really nervous, and the only way to calm those nerves is to see and reassure the other, then that is what you must do. Go with your gut feeling rather than tradition on this one.

Wedding morning checklist

1 Do you have your buttonhole?

2 Has the best man got the rings?

3 Do you have your change of clothes for the next day?

4 Has the luggage for your first night and honeymoon – including documents, tickets and passports – been delivered to your first-night hotel or stowed in the car boot?

5 Do you have some spare change in case of an emergency?

6 Do you have a crib sheet of events?

7 Your speech notes?

8 The thank-you gifts?

9 Your going-away car keys, if you're driving?

What happens on the day?

Church wedding

At a church wedding, the bridegroom and the best man should arrive about half an hour before the service, to await the arrival of the bride, either in the vestry or seated in the front pew on the right-hand side of the church.

At a given signal, the bridegroom takes his place at the chancel step before the altar, with the best man standing to his right. Then your future wife will begin that long, long walk up the aisle.

Once you are officially husband and wife, with your bride on your left arm you proceed to the vestry for the signing of the register. After receiving congratulations and greetings from both sides and when the bride is ready, you again give her your left arm and together you lead the bridal procession down the aisle.

Be prepared to have photographs taken for up to an hour (or sometimes more) after the ceremony and during the first part of the reception.

Civil ceremonies

Much the same procedure is followed in a civil wedding, which can be much simpler or just as ceremonious, depending on what you and the bride have decided. See also pages 36–39.

Organizing the wedding cars
The bride will normally travel in a car with her father (or
whoever is giving her away). All the bridesmaids and the
mother of the bride will travel in another car (or two if they
won't all fit in one). They leave for the ceremony before the
bride and her father. The groom will usually travel to church
with the best man. This can be in either a hire car or in one of
their own. The ushers usually meet the groom and best man at
the church, as they have to make sure they are the first people
there. The parents of the bride should remember to make
arrangements for getting home from the reception in the
evening, if need be!

At the reception

As the groom, you should welcome your guests as they arrive at the reception and mingle with them, introducing your bride to any members of your family and friends whom she has not already met. Or you may stand in a formal receiving line to greet guests individually.

The receiving line

A receiving line is a line formed by you, your wife and often both sets of parents so that you can all be properly introduced, in turn, to everyone at the reception and each guest is welcomed. It can take place either as people arrive at the venue or as they make their way into the dining room if drinks are being served first. It is becoming increasingly popular for a master of ceremonies to announce each guest as they enter the room, so everyone in the receiving line knows who they are about to speak to.

Some couples prefer to greet guests on their own, but if parents are in the receiving line, it is advisable to go through the guest list with them before the day so that everyone is acquainted with the guests' names.

Traditionally, the order of people in the line is as follows: bride's mother, bride's father, groom's mother, groom's father, bride, groom. The bride's mother and father come first, as traditionally they are the hosts, although not always.

If you have lots of guests it's a good idea to keep the receiving line as short as possible. Having just the two of you greeting guests will prevent long queues.

The groom's speech

The bridegroom is supposed to reply to the toast to 'the bride and groom', proposed by the bride's father. The primary purpose of your speech is to say thank you to the bride's parents for their daughter and for the wedding, thank you to your parents, thank you to your bride, thank you to everyone who has contributed to the wedding or supported you in some way, and thank you to your guests.

Giving gifts

It is traditional for the bride and groom to present a gift to their mothers, usually flowers, during the speeches. This is a way of saying 'thank you for being my mother', rather than a gift for what they may have contributed to the wedding.

Gifts are also given to the best man (and sometimes the ushers) and the bridesmaids. Cufflinks are a popular choice for the best man and ushers, while jewellery is often given to bridesmaids, but it could be any kind of memento of the wedding day. It is also traditional for the bride and groom to exchange presents on the day or the day before the wedding.

Etiquette corner: Toastmasters

Do we need a toastmaster, and what would he or she do during the reception?

You may choose to employ a professional toastmaster (or master of ceremonies) to conduct the reception, introducing the bride and groom as they enter the reception as well as the speeches. He or she would also introduce each event of the celebrations, such as the receiving line, the serving of the meal, the cutting of the cake, and the first dance. In the absence of a toastmaster, the best man should introduce the speeches.

After your speech

The cutting of the cake

The cutting of the cake usually follows the last speech, which is traditionally the best man's. Some couples choose to combine cake with dessert and cut it before the speeches. If you want your guests to witness this, the best time would be as soon as everyone is settled at the reception, when the welcome drinks are handed out. This way you allow your caterers enough time to prepare the cake as dessert.

If you are going to use your cake as dessert, why not consider an alternative to traditional fruitcake, such as chocolate cake or *croquembouche*?

You may find some of your older guests like to take their wedding cake home, so it's nice to keep a little back. It's also traditional to send a piece of cake to guests who couldn't attend, to show you were thinking of them.

The first dance

When the band kicks in, the first on the dance floor should be the newlyweds. Then the rest of the party joins in, with the groom dancing with his new mother-in-law and the bride with her father. The bride then dances with her father-in-law and the groom with his mother. Finally, the groom and the chief bridesmaid take to the floor, while the bride and best man dance. If you're not a great mover, or feel uncomfortable about dancing in public, open the dance floor to everyone as soon as the music begins.

Partying all night long

If you're being ultra-traditional, you and your bride will disappear later in the evening to change, to reappear to say goodbye to guests before 'going away' on your honeymoon.

However, most couples now don't follow the tradition of leaving their reception early – why waste a great party? If you plan to party until the bitter end, be polite and warn your older guests. They were brought up to think it rude to leave a reception before the bride and groom!

A lovely farewell when you leave the reception is for the guests who've still got the stamina to create a 'tunnel' of arched hands for you to pass under. This way you get to say goodbye to all your guests – a reverse receiving line!

If you are staying at the party until the end, book your first night's accommodation locally. You might want to plan a surprise such as candles, soft music, champagne or flowers.

Etiquette corner: Evening guests

How do we make evening guests feel as welcome as the day guests?

If you've invited a number of friends to the evening part of your reception only, it's important to make sure that they have a good time. With so much to arrange for the ceremony and the main part of the reception, it's easy to assume that they will simply join in with the party. But there are a few things that you can do to ensure that the new guests feel welcome and relaxed.

- Work out what time you expect the meal and speeches to end and ask your evening guests to arrive no earlier than 45 minutes later. This will allow time to clear away the meal and set up the music, if you're having any. Encourage your day guests to move from their seats and mingle, perhaps moving to a new drinking and dancing area.
- If space is limited, move the main tables aside. This will make it easier for your evening guests to blend into the party.
- Wait until your second wave of guests has arrived before you cut the cake. This is a simple way to include your evening guests in the more traditional part of your reception.

The honeymoon

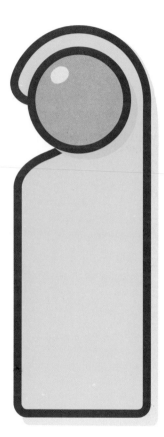

Planning, booking and paying for the honeymoon is usually the groom's responsibility, and for a honeymoon to remember – for the best reasons – it's worth taking time to get it right.

However, for many couples, planning the trip of a lifetime is one of the most exciting parts of the pre-wedding experience and something they can do without family interference. So even if you research it, make it a joint venture with your bride and enjoy it together. Many couples now also share the costs of the honeymoon.

If you are planning a surprise trip, make sure you give your bride an idea of what to expect so that she will know what to pack and can plan to have all the necessary documentation and vaccinations.

It takes two

What do you **both** want to do? Make sure that neither of you is simply agreeing to two weeks on a beach to keep the other happy. Remember, too, that you don't have to follow other people's preconceptions about honeymoons. 'Whatever makes you happy' is truly the key. So, if playing Scrabble together is what you really enjoy, don't worry that it isn't romantic enough – just do it.

Do think about money (see budgeting, page 16). In many ways, it's far better to choose a honeymoon that you can easily afford and have enough spending money once you're actually there rather than having to count your pennies all the time.

Great honeymoon destinations

As soon as you have set your wedding date, turn your attention to the honeymoon. You should aim to book it as soon as possible, especially if you're getting married during a peak holiday season.

If you're about to splash out on a 'once-in-a-lifetime' trip, you might even want to set the honeymoon date first. Bear in mind that, although the majority of British weddings take place in June, July and August, this may not be the best time to travel to your chosen destination.

Honeymoon options

- If all you're really after is a quiet, relaxing time together and the stress of long-haul flights isn't your scene, then a remote cottage in Britain may serve you far better than an expensive, all-inclusive, Far Eastern beach holiday.
- If you want something glamorous and gorgeous, then saving on travel expenses in favour of a top-class location may be the best bet. For example, take the train to France then stay in a succession of luxurious châteaux and hotels.
- For a taste of adventure choose an African safari, white-water rafting, diving or trekking. Just make sure you book through a reputable company and that any dangerous activities are properly supervised.
- Perhaps you can think of nothing more romantic than being in St Mark's Square, Venice, or seeing the pyramids. Make sure you know what you can visit and when.

- Walking hand-in-hand through the surf on a white sandy beach is surely the definitive honeymoon scene. Just be sure – especially if you are active types – that you really do both want to be lazing around for the duration of your stay; or choose a resort where you can build in some separate activities, such as scuba diving.
- An activity element – perhaps walking, skiing or cycling – can be perfect if you both love the activity involved. After all the stress of the wedding – and all that food and drink – some decent exercise can be invigorating and restorative.
- The most popular honeymoon choice nowadays is a 'two-centre' break, combining a week of beach-based romantic relaxation with a more active or city-based week.
- Two's company... Think carefully before inviting family and friends along on your honeymoon – this is a very special time in your married life and you won't get it again.

Budget or bust

Don't underestimate how exhausted you'll be once the wedding is over. You'll need a good break and it's worth paying a little more to stay somewhere decent. For this reason, last-minute bargain breaks are not really a good idea, unless you really don't mind when and where the honeymoon takes place! Planning well in advance may cost a bit more, but it means you'll get what you really want, when you want it.

Don't add extra stress to the trip by leaving too many elements to chance. Delays are more likely on chartered flights, so you're better off spending your money on scheduled flights instead. You don't want to spend your first night as husband and wife in a departure lounge! Book at least the first week's accommodation up front, plan the itinerary and book your car hire or internal flights. You can even plan and book activities, such as city tours or scuba diving, in advance. Search online for the local tourist board and get some ideas of what you can do while you're away.

- Travel insurance is important for peace of mind. Should one of you fall ill, or a theft occur, you'll be covered. Make sure your policy covers the value of your wedding and engagement rings.
- If you're marrying abroad as well, take out a special wedding policy, that will cover your wedding outfits and gifts.
- Build lots of spending money into your budget, so you can indulge in a little luxury. There's not much difference between a four- and five-star hotel – spend the money you save on having fun.

Honeymoon checklist

Three months before the wedding

- By this time you should have booked any flights/package holidays and arranged travel insurance.
- Draw up a basic itinerary and book at least the first few days' accommodation.
- Make sure your passports are valid. If you are changing your name and want to travel in your married name, contact the passport office for the necessary forms to complete.
- Obtain visas, if required.
- Have all the necessary vaccinations and check whether you need to take malaria tablets.

One month before the wedding

- Finalize your itinerary, pre-book activities, if desired, and confirm hotels in writing.
- Arrange transport from your first-night hotel to the airport and from the airport to home on your return, if applicable.

- Order your foreign currency and travellers' cheques.
- Collect all the necessary paperwork (tickets, passports, addresses and phone numbers of hotels, driver's licence, insurance details) and file it together in a safe place.
- Plan your packing.
- Arrange for someone to collect your wedding clothes from the first-night hotel and store them, or return them to the hire shops.
- Make arrangements for someone to look after your wedding presents – honeymooning newlyweds are often prime targets for break-ins.

One week before the wedding

- Collect your currency and travellers' cheques.

One day before the wedding

- Pack and have your luggage taken to the first-night hotel or other convenient point for collection.

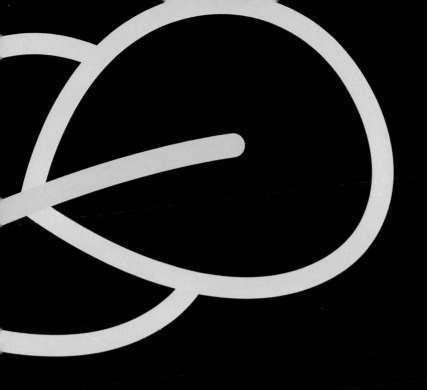

Writing your
speech

The groom's speech

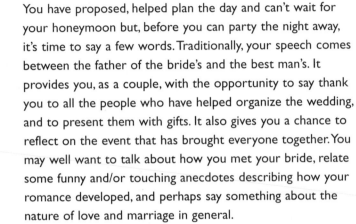

You have proposed, helped plan the day and can't wait for your honeymoon but, before you can party the night away, it's time to say a few words. Traditionally, your speech comes between the father of the bride's and the best man's. It provides you, as a couple, with the opportunity to say thank you to all the people who have helped organize the wedding, and to present them with gifts. It also gives you a chance to reflect on the event that has brought everyone together. You may well want to talk about how you met your bride, relate some funny and/or touching anecdotes describing how your romance developed, and perhaps say something about the nature of love and marriage in general.

You will say the most important words of the day, if not your life, when you say 'I do'. Now it's your chance to thank everybody and tell your bride how much you love her, and in front of everybody you know. Daunted? Don't be – everybody is there because they want to be. They've chosen to spend their free time watching you marry the woman you love and, for once, the focus is not on her dress but on you.

For many grooms, the speech can cause something of a dilemma. On one hand, a wedding is the occasion for expressing love for your new wife and gratitude to both sets of parents but, on the other hand, you may not want to come across as too sentimental in front of friends! Therefore, it would be helpful to plan your speech as a happy medium between the two.

Remember that if your bride is not going to give a speech, all your words should be from both of you. Bear this in mind throughout your speech – you don't want to just include your new wife in a single section of it as if you'd only just remembered to bung her in at the last minute! Oh – and beginning your speech 'My wife and I...' usually provokes an immediate audience reaction!

Your speech

Few people are practised in the art of public speaking, so the thought of standing up in front of everyone at a wedding reception and sounding good is pretty intimidating. But don't panic. We have all the advice you need for preparing and making your speech.

Who speaks and when

Traditionally, the toastmaster or master of ceremonies will introduce the speeches at the end of the meal, but some couples now decide to have the speeches beforehand to allow the speakers to enjoy their meal free of nerves. The formal order of speakers is:

- Father of the bride (or a close family friend)
- The groom
- The best man

If the bride, chief bridesmaid or guests want to speak, that's great, too!

The basics

- First, don't panic. A little careful planning will help you deliver a speech that you'll be proud of.
- At the reception venue, get an idea of where you'll be standing and the size of the room.
- You will need to project your voice, so practise speaking out loud.
- Is the reception going to have a theme that you could refer to in your speech or incorporate into it?
- Think carefully about whether there are any subjects you should avoid.
- How many guests will there be? As a general rule, the more people present, the more formal the speech.

Where to start

So, what is expected of the groom?

- The first task is to thank your new father-in-law for his speech and for his beautiful daughter.
- Thank the guests for sharing your day and for their generous gifts.
- Thank both sets of parents for their help with the wedding celebrations.
- Give a small gift to the two mothers (for some suggestions, see www.confetti.co.uk).
- Compliment your new wife!
- Thank the best man for his help, and give your gifts to him and to the rest of the bridal party.
- Raise a glass and offer a toast to the bridesmaids.

Making it funny

First of all, relax. You're planning a wedding speech, not a slot as a stand-up comedian. A few jokes spread judiciously through your speech will be more than enough. This is one of the few times in life when you can be guaranteed a captive and sympathetic audience. If you're planning to deliver your speech after the meal, then most of the guests will have had at least a glass or two of wine, so they'll be relaxed and in the mood for a laugh. Remember, just be yourself because, after all, it's the real you that everyone wants to hear from.

Everyone will be on your side and ready to laugh at even the slightest attempt at humour, so help them. Check early on that everyone can hear you. No one will laugh at something they can't hear, so speak clearly and don't gabble. Signal jokes by pausing to allow everyone to laugh! Keep the gags short and if the joke fails, then make the failure the joke.

Props

Well-chosen physical gags can work wonders. At one
wedding, a best man known for his emotional outbursts
threw out packs of paper tissues to everyone in preparation.
(Sure enough, he was crying five minutes later – so they all
got thrown back!)

Finally...

Keep your speech short. Less is definitely more – and brevity
is most definitely the soul of wit.

Don't try too hard – a heartfelt, affectionate speech that
raise smiles is much better than an OTT, hammy performance
that causes the entire wedding party to cringe.

Speech taboos

Wedding speeches should be memorable. But make sure that guests remember your speech for the right reasons. Bear in mind that causing offence in your wedding speech could be preserved forever on video, as well as in the minds of the guests! Here's what NOT to do...

Cardinal sins

- Avoid certain subjects such as race and religious issues, ex-partners, relatives who refused to attend, the last-minute threat to call off the wedding.
- Keep in mind that you have a mixed audience. If an anecdote can't easily be explained, leave it out.
- Swear words are a definite no-go area. The last thing you need is granny fainting at a four-letter word.
- Don't forget to thank everyone you need to thank.
- Don't ramble – long speeches are likely to send older guests off to the land of nod, so keep it short.

- Don't skip all over the place: have a definite beginning, middle and end.
- Try not to mumble, swallow your words, speak too fast or lose your place (in which case you may as well admit it and get a laugh).
- Don't ad-lib your speech, unless you are very, very good at it.
- Tempting though it is to drink heavily to steady your nerves, don't get wasted. Adrenaline can increase the effect of alcohol, and any evidence on videos and photos will haunt you forever.

Structure and delivery

Planning your speech

It can be daunting when faced with a blank piece of paper and the need to write your wedding day speech. Remember that all wedding speeches are just extended toasts, so don't worry that yours has to be worthy of an Oscar winner. Keep your speech quite brief – about five minutes is a good length of time.

Start by noting suitable headings to focus on, then fill in the spaces to produce an entire speech (see also page 67). Make your speech relevant to all the guests and have a definite beginning ('Ladies and gentlemen...'); a middle (a set list of stories and topics in a clear and logical order); and an end (your final words leading up to the toast). Have a look on the Internet for some ideas.

The biggest aid to overcoming nerves when speaking in public is to be confident that you're well prepared, so write out your speech clearly and concisely in BIG BOLD CAPITALS, keeping the sentences short and clear. Alternatively, compile a list of bullet points to prompt you, even if you have memorized your speech completely.

Success on the day

- Try not to let the speech dominate your thoughts and stop you enjoying the occasion.
- Avoid too much alcohol before your speech, as it may cloud your judgement or make you slur your words.
- If you're concerned that your voice will not carry very well, ask one of the ushers or a member of the venue staff to stand at the back of the room when you start your speech and indicate if they can't hear you.
- Begin your speech by taking a deep breath and smiling, if at all possible!
- Adrenaline will carry you to the end of your speech before you know it. If you make a mistake, smile, correct yourself and continue.
- Remember to speak slowly. If you feel yourself racing away, stop, take a deep breath and then continue.
- Try to enjoy yourself as you make your speech and think of the meaning behind your words, so that everyone is clear of your feelings for those you're speaking about.
- Having done all of this, relax and enjoy the applause, and the rest of the day!

Tips for a good speech

- Take time to think about what you want to say and who you need to thank. Get into the habit of carrying a notebook around with you so you can jot down any thoughts. The best ideas often come to you at the most unlikely moments...

- Break down your words into the different areas you want to cover, such as who you need to thank and what you want to say about your new wife. Take the jottings from your notebook and see where they fit into the plan.

- Anxiety about losing the text of your speech can ruin a whole wedding morning. Make three or four copies of the final version and give one to three or four guests to look after. It's impossible for all the copies to be lost — and it will put your mind at rest!

- Make eye contact ... but not with everyone at once! Speak as if you were talking to one person, and address them directly. Of course, you will want to look around the room, but take time to focus on one person at a time.

- Remember that everyone is rooting for you! This is your wedding and, although the scale of the occasion might initially seem daunting, it is in many ways the easiest public speaking opportunity of all. Everyone is on your side and no one wants you to do badly.

- Read your speech out again and again – preferably to other people. Making a recording of yourself can be useful, too. Listen out for places where you speak too fast or where the point you're making is unclear, and revise your speech accordingly.

- Make sure your speech will mean something to everyone present. There may be guests who know only half of the wedding party so anecdotes should be told in such a way that everyone can enjoy them.

- Don't rely on your memory. You may have practised your speech so hard that you're sure you know it by heart. Keep your text handy anyway – the stress of public speaking can sometimes cause people to forget their lines.

- Time your speech and stick to it – five minutes is about right. Keep jokes and anecdotes short, so that if one doesn't work, you can swiftly move on to the next. And don't laugh at your own jokes – you'll soon know whether you've scored a hit!

- Although to you your speech is something written, to your guests it is something spoken. So make sure your language is not too stiff or formal. Change all the 'could nots' to 'couldn'ts', and make free with the first person!

- In most people's minds, the word 'speech' is associated with great tension, formality and the need to perform well. But thinking of it instead as part of a conversation at a largish dinner party, or simply as a few words to wish some friends well, will make the whole thing seem less intimidating.

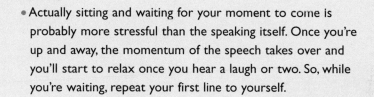

- Actually sitting and waiting for your moment to come is probably more stressful than the speaking itself. Once you're up and away, the momentum of the speech takes over and you'll start to relax once you hear a laugh or two. So, while you're waiting, repeat your first line to yourself.

- There are traditions and customs about who should speak and what they should say but, if it suits you, feel free to ignore any or all of them. So, if you want to give only a brief toast to those who helped organize the wedding rather than a long spiel, or want to give a speech with your wife, fine. Give the speech on your own terms and you'll achieve the best result.

- When speaking or reading in public, people have a marked tendency to rush their words without realizing it. So, it's a good idea to insert the word 'pause' at intervals in your speech or, if you're using cue cards, to insert blank cards that will automatically slow you down.

- Whenever the speeches are scheduled to take place – at the end of the meal is the norm – make sure that nothing else is going on and that all the clearing up has stopped. Speakers need everyone's undivided attention!

Useful phrases and ideas

Father-in-law, guests

Here are some useful phrases and ideas for a great groom's speech. All you need to do is pick the best ones for you and fill in the blanks!

Thank your new father-in-law

- I just want to thank my father-in-law for his *kind/generous/special words*. I feel honoured that he has *taken/welcomed* me into his family.

- Thank you, Ken, for your *kind/generous/sweet/special words*. It is good to know how you feel about Sarah and me getting married.

- My wife and I would like to thank Ken for being the best father of the bride ever. Not only did he give her away instead of locking her in her room, but his *kind/sweet/generous/witty* words have also made me feel welcome as the newest member of his family.

- My wife and I want to thank Ken for his *witty/kind/generous/sincere words*. I now feel *embarrassed about everything I said about him in the past/justified in my opinion that he's a great/good/perfect* father-in-law. What can I say after that speech? Thanks, Ken.

Thank your guests

- This is the most important day of our lives, and *my wife and I/Sarah and I/we* are delighted to share it with *so many friends and family/our closest friends and families/two complete strangers in a register office.* We are also very grateful that so many of you have not only gone to the expense of sharing this day with us but have also bought us presents. Thank you.

- I can't believe that you all made it here. You really are the best *bunch/group/lot/mob/pack/herd* of friends and family that we could ever hope to have. So thank you. We're also extremely grateful for the presents. Sarah was saying only a couple of days ago that she really wanted another toaster... or two!

Thank you

Useful phrases and ideas

In-laws, wife, bride

Thank your in-laws

- I am so *delighted/pleased/honoured/relieved/happy* to have **Ken and Angela** as my *new family/in-laws/other Mum and Dad.* I knew that I'd *like/love/get on with/adore* them when I fell in love with **Sarah** because they have helped her to be the person she is – *perfect/rich/wonderful/fond of beer and rugby!*

Compliment your wife!

- You are always beautiful but you have never looked as *stunning/good/wonderful/gorgeous* as you do today. You make the most *wonderful/stunning/gorgeous/perfect bride.* I love you.

- I was expecting to feel *nervous/sick/terrified/ concerned/worried/frightened* when I woke up today but I didn't. Why? Because I knew that you would be walking down that aisle towards me and that the only thing I wanted was for *you to be my wife/us to be married.* I knew that you would look lovely – you always do – but today you are *radiant/gorgeous/beautiful/ wonderful/fantastic/ stunning/a vision/perfect/the perfect bride.* You mean so much to me, and I want to thank you for agreeing to become my wife. I am so *proud/happy/honoured* to be your husband, and I love you very much.

- Sarah, you are a *beautiful/stunning/radiant/gorgeous/ lovely bride*, and I know that you are just as beautiful on the inside. When we first met, I realized that you *were the most beautiful woman in the world/were the only woman for me/had a ladder in your stockings*, but I never *thought/imagined/dared to hope* that you would marry me. I am so *happy/chuffed/delighted/ecstatic* that you agreed to be my wife and share the rest of your life with me. I've been so proud of the way you have juggled organizing this wedding with *everything else/your job* and have still been understanding and patient. Now, I just want to say, in front of our friends and family, how much you mean to me. I love you.

Thank your bride

- I never thought I could be as happy as I am today without *England/Wales/Scotland/Ireland* winning the Six Nations. Roz, you've made me feel like I've *scored the winning try/kicked a critical drop goal* in the match of my life. You're my *Twickenham/Millennium Stadium/ Murrayfield/Lansdowne Road*, and right now I feel like cheering because I'm just over the moon you've married me. I know there will be times when you send me *for an early bath/to sit in the sin bin*. But I also know that, just like supporting Bath, it's something that stays with you for life, through the ups and downs, and you just can't change that. Roz, I'm your biggest fan, and I love you.

(You can amend the above to reflect your favourite sport – but only use it if it's not a sore spot with the bride!)

Useful phrases and ideas
Best man, bridesmaids

Thank the best man

- When I asked Sarah to marry me, I knew that I needed a best man and that there was only one man that title could be given to. Bob *is my brother and also a friend/has been my best friend since school/1972/we met in the sandpit/he stole my BMX*, and I knew that he would be perfect for the job. I would like to thank him for all the work he's done today – *acting as toastmaster/not losing the rings/getting me to the church on time/finding my trousers* – and for his efforts before the wedding when he listened to me as I raved about the latest *waistcoat/buttonhole/wedding dress* I had seen. Bob, you've been *great/a mate/the best man I could have chosen/cool/a pal/a true friend/gorgeous*!

- I get the fun parts of today, but Bob has all the stressful parts. As he's the *local postie/hippo-keeper/accountant/general layabout*, I knew that he would be more than able to cope with today and keep everything, especially me, ticking along smoothly.

Thank and toast the bridesmaids

- The *giggling little posse/stunning group* of beautiful bridesmaids *over there/to my right/to my left/in front of you* have been amazing. Not only did they manage to walk down the aisle without falling over, but they've

also been great with all the preparations. It may seem unfair to the rest of you, as you've all been *so great/ helpful/ amazing/bored rigid*, but I'd particularly like to thank Vikki for all her hard work. I understand that Sarah's dress would not be looking quite so *beautiful/stunning/together/white* as it does now were it not for a timely intervention! Ladies and gentleman, I'd like you all to charge/raise your glasses. I give you... the bridesmaids.

• *My wife and I/Sarah and I* would like to say a special thank you to the bridesmaids, who have been a tower of strength throughout the *preparations/day*. They've been *great/wonderful/beautiful*, and little Anna has been so *good/patient/sweet* and looks *gorgeous/adorable/very grown up* in her dress. Ladies and gentlemen, please *charge/raise* your glasses.
I give you... the bridesmaids.

Jokes
and one-liners

Making a humorous speech

Stuck for a witticism to fill out your epic speech? Why not pick some jokes or one-liners from the selection here, all of which are based on real wedding speeches and toasts. Not every line will fit exactly the speech or toast you're planning, of course, but hopefully you'll find an idea you can adapt, a line you can make your own.

As you prepare your words, remember not to try too hard. You don't have to be a stand-up comedian, just someone who's put a little time, care and thought into your speech...

How to be funny

Every speaker wants to raise the roof – or at least a few smiles. Don't feel under pressure to be funny. Remember that everyone's on your side and they want your words to work as much as you do.

- **Establish a rapport with your audience** Refer to something topical that all present can relate to: 'Phew! I don't know about you but I thought I was going to keel over in that church...'

- **Nervous?** Don't panic. Make a gag about Imodium or jelly legs!

- **Try and enjoy yourself** Or at least look like you are. It'll help to relax the room.

- **Keep it simple** If you have to explain the gag, you're doing it wrong!

- **Practice makes perfect** Test out your speech on friends and colleagues, note their reactions and amend as necessary.

- **Think of your whole audience and be sensitive** Avoid private in-jokes, technical jargon and anything that might offend granny.

- **Be brief** Even the best speech can become a yawn if it goes on for too long.

- **Jokes aren't everything** A few words spoken from the heart can be just as effective.

What the experts say

'The more you practise delivering your speech, the less nervous you will be. Practise the pauses, the intonations, the anecdotes... Recite your speech in the shower. On the bus. On the loo. On the night, your nerves will thank you, because instead of fretting about the audience or your flies, you'll simply focus on what you're going to say.'

Rob Pointer, stand-up comic

'Don't speak when you're looking down at your notes. Look down for a moment, look up, smile at everyone, speak – then repeat. You don't need to talk constantly; it gives guests a break, and if you're not afraid of silence, you'll look confident, so everyone can relax. Remember that in between speaking, silence feels approximately ten times longer than it is, so take it nice and slow.'

Jill Edwards, comedy coach and scriptwriter

Lines that work – and lines that don't...

Always a winner

- 'Not for the first time today do I rise from a warm seat clutching a piece of paper...'
- 'And so without further ado, let's raise our glasses...'
- 'I'm sure you'll agree that I'm the luckiest man in the world today.'
- 'I do!'

Definite no-nos

- 'Frankly, I'm amazed we've got this far without my parents coming to blows...'
- Any reference to bridal pregnancy (except by prior agreement).
- References to the cost of the wedding.

Good for a groan

- 'Unaccustomed as I am to public speaking...'
- 'My wife and I...'

Bride

Age gap

'People often ask us if the age gap between me and Janine has a big impact on our relationship. And I always say [shouting, cupping ear with hand]: "WHAT'S THAT? CAN YOU SPEAK UP, DEAR? YES, LOVELY WEATHER WE'VE BEEN HAVING..."

Bathroom habits

'I won't say that Lyn likes to spend a long time getting ready in the bathroom, but usually by the time I've waited for her to come out, I need to shave again.'

First time we met

[After a protracted engagement] 'I knew at once that I had made a big impression on Cath, because shortly after that first fateful meeting, she *went and left the country for three months/started dating my flatmate/converted to Christianity/joined Narcotics Anonymous/took to meditating every night/did a First Aid course!*'

Housework

'In our house, I promise my wife here and now, before everyone present, that I will not treat "wash", "cook" and "iron" as four-letter words.'

New man

'I'll never forget the day Anne told me I was going to marry her...'

Birthdays

'As some of you may know, today is my birthday. At the risk of sounding corny, let me just say that my new wife is the best present anyone could wish for.'

Drinking habits

'I wouldn't say Louisa has a drinking problem, but I did once catch her trying to down a bottle of aftershave. "What on earth are you doing that for?" I asked, "I thought it was eau de cologne," she replied.'

Engagement

'I wouldn't say my parents were "pleasantly surprised" when I told them that Jean had accepted my hand in marriage. "Pleasantly gobsmacked" would be much more like it.'

Relatives

Birthdays

'Today, for those of you who don't know, it also happens to be the father of the bride's birthday. What rotten luck – having to buy everyone the first round at the bar on top of everything else he's spent today!'

Children

'I'd like to say a big thank you to my one-year-old nephew Paul, without whose constant help and attention this wedding would have been prepared in half the time.'

First impressions

'The first time I met my future parents-in-law, I choked on a tea cake, stepped on the cat and smashed a French window as the result of an over-energetic game of swingball. But it wasn't all plain sailing. Let me tell you about some of the sticky moments...'

In-laws

'In Dave and Pippa I have gained the perfect in-laws. I always cringe when I hear jokes about difficult mothers-in-law because my own experience has been so far from that stereotype. [Pause, turn to in-laws timorously] Did I read that right?'

Mothers-in-law

'What can I tell you about Paula? So fond am I of my mother-in-law, in fact, that I barely consider her to be my mother-in-law at all...'

Mum

'Possibly the only person more delighted to see me get married today is my Mum. When I was single and I went to a friend's wedding, she'd ask me all about it afterwards. Then, slowly clearing away the tea things, she'd say something like, "She must have been so proud, the groom's mother." The chin starts to wobble slightly. And then: "I only hope I'm still around when – if – you ever get married." Thanks for not putting on the pressure, Mum!'

Ushers

'I'd just like to apologize if you were one of the many people my brother-in-law Jack loudly told to "SHUT IT!" during the service. He thinks that's what the usher's job is.'

Wives

'If girls are inclined to marry men just like their fathers, is that why so many mothers cry at weddings?'

Jobs, interests and best man

Jobs

'On behalf of all my colleagues here today, I would like to say that there is no truth in the rumour that actuaries are people who found accountancy too exciting.'

'OK, so during the week my *bride/Dad/best man works as a tax inspector/estate agent/traffic warden*. But I'm glad to say that *she/he* is here today in *her/his* off-duty capacity as a *blushing bride/proud father/loving human being...*'

Interests

'Golf has been a passion of mine for as long as I can remember, but I'm afraid that June's never really got into it. The one time she came along, as she landed in a bunker for the third hole running, I asked her if she wanted a sand wedge. She said: "Ooooh lovely – have you got any tuna and cucumber?"'

'Eve is obsessed with India. On our first date we went to a Bollywood karaoke bar, and on our second to the latest Bollywood film. I've promised her that I will help her fulfil her dream of visiting the Taj Mahal. I don't care how much it costs: it's the best restaurant in Peckham and it's worth every penny...'

'Jen loves everything to do with keep fit: water aerobics, spinning, pilates, cross-training, step aerobics... you name it, she does it. When we started living together, I soon discovered that we had rather different ideas of what constitutes a "Sunday morning workout".'

Best man

'As you may know, the best man is currently single. He's in the enviable position of being able to marry anyone he pleases; all he's got to do now is find one he pleases. In fact, more and more women are choosing not to get married; he knows this, because they've all told him. He's looking for a woman who'll be able to take a joke. Well, it's the only kind he'll get...'

'It's been great – if highly unusual – to see the best man and all the ushers dressed up in morning suits today. And if any of the bridesmaids are available and chocoholics, just think of the old advertising slogan, "P-p-p-p-pick up a penguin".'

Wedding gifts

'Looking at all the wonderful gifts we've received today, I'm reminded of the story of the couple who got engaged when they were both in their 90s. They went for a stroll to discuss their wedding plans, and wandered into a big chemist's. "Excuse me," asked the couple. "Do you sell heart medication?"

"Yes," said the pharmacist.

"What about rheumatism cream?"

"Oh yes."

"Viagra?"

"Yes, sir."

"Vitamins and sleeping pills?"

"Most certainly."

"Indigestion tablets and denture cleanser?"

"All kinds." The couple looked at each other excitedly.

"Are you thinking what I'm thinking?" said the man.

"Oh yes," said the woman. So they turned back to the pharmacist and said: "We'd like to have our wedding list here, please."'

'Ladies and gentlemen, I'd like to thank you for all the many gifts you have so kindly given us today. There they all sit, piled up on that big table over there. I'm glad to say that we haven't received three toasters or 15 candle sets. I know this already without unwrapping them because, like Darth Vader, I can feel your presents...'

Jokes

'A man walks into a dentist's and says: "You've got to help me. I think I'm a moth." The dentist says: "To be quite frank, I don't think I can help. What you need is a psychiatrist. Why did you come in here anyway?" The man replies: "Well, the light was on."'

'A man walks into a doctor's surgery completely wrapped in clingfilm. "Before you say anything," says the doctor, "I can clearly see you're nuts!"'

'A naughty inflatable student is summoned to see the inflatable headmaster of an inflatable school. "That drawing pin incident," the headmaster began. "Not only have you let yourself down, you've let me down, you've let the whole school down."'

'Two women meet at a party. "Isn't your ring on the wrong finger?" asks one. "I know," says the other. "I married the wrong man."'

'What do you call a sheep with no legs?
A cloud.'

'Husband: "Why do you keep studying the wedding licence?"
Wife: "I'm looking for loopholes."'

'A little girl spies her pregnant mum and asks her why
her tummy is so big. "There's a baby in there," says her
mum. "Where did it come from?" asks the little girl,
persistently. "Daddy gave it to me." So the little girl
goes and sees her dad. "Daddy, Daddy," she says. "You
know that baby you gave to Mummy?"
"Yeees," says Dad, a little embarrassed. "Well," sighs
the little girl, "She's only gone and eaten it."'

'Mrs Werewolf: "Hello dear, how was your day?"
Mr Werewolf (just home from work, very moody):
"Leave me alone! I don't want to talk about it!"
Mrs Werewolf (spotting full moon out of the window):
"Oh dear. Is it that time of the month already?"'

'Why do female black widow spiders kill their partners
after mating?
To stop the snoring before it starts.'

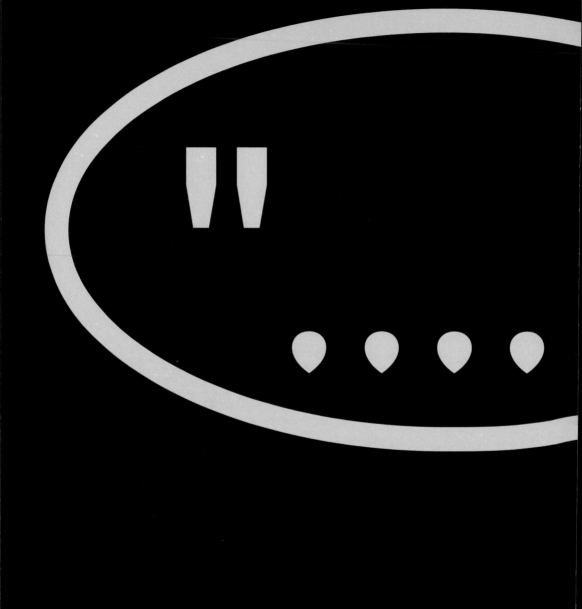

Great
sample
speeches

The groom's speech

Traditionally, the groom's speech includes lots of thank yous – to your father-in-law for his speech, to the guests for coming and for their gifts, to your parents for their help with the celebrations and for being your parents, and to your new wife.

There may well be others you may want to thank for their contribution, from the person who made the dresses to the baker of the wedding cake to the ushers. Now is the moment.

The groom's speech goes on to end with more thanks – to the best man (often with a plea for leniency) and a toast to the bridesmaids.

That may be as much as you want to say – which is absolutely fine – or you may want to work in an additional theme, for instance on the ups and downs of your wedding plans, the difference in age between you and the bride, or even your nerves about speaking.

Our first sample speech gives some suggestions for how to go through your thank yous, while the rest of the speeches here provide some ideas for themes to take your speech further.

Sample speech 1

Thank you, thank you

'Ladies and gents, boys and girls, I'd like to begin by thanking my new father-in-law for his very kind words and extending a big warm welcome to everyone.

'It's lovely to see you all here, at the end of what's been another fabulous week for sales of Diocalm and Imodium [cough nervously and rub belly].

'Some of you, we know, have come a long way to be here today: we have guests from Plymouth, from Yorkshire, even [point to guests] France. *Bienvenus, les grenouilles.* (It's OK, they can't understand my accent.)

'And my nephew Sam has even come all the way back from his teaching job in Xi'an in China to be with us today. Ni-Hao Sam! You can check out Sam in action later this evening when he'll be spinning the platters that matter as one of our resident DJs. I just hope you all like deep-core techno-jungle...

'Then, of course, one or two of you have even struggled all the way up the hill from Archway and from Crouch End, a distance of some two or three miles.

'We're so glad you all made it. It really does mean the world to us both to see you all here.

'As many of you will know, Eve and I met by a trivia machine in a pub called the Camden Head. What's less well-known is that Eve actually won me as a booby prize for getting a question wrong about Arsenal.

'Ever since that first auspicious meeting, I've been ushered into a wonderful world of new experiences and sensations.

'I'll never forget my first viewing of *Monsoon Wedding* (sadly, by no means the last); the unexpected pleasure of hearing the same Country Classics album 25 times in a row; or the day I discovered from my green-fingered wife the meaning of the verb... to mulch. (I wouldn't say that my wife is obsessed with gardening, but she's the only bride I know who beamed on her wedding day when it started raining.)

'But in coming to terms with all these strange new experiences, I can honestly say that I've loved every single minute. My life has been enriched in 1,000 different ways since I met Eve, and I cannot believe how lucky I am to have her as my companion and my guide. I don't care how many times you've heard this before... but today I really am the luckiest man alive.

'My wife and I would like to say a huge thank you to everyone who's helped put this day together.

'Most of all, we'd like to thank our parents, not just for everything they've done for us today but also for the love and support they have given us day in, day out, throughout our whole lives.

'(And I know how much my dear Dad would have loved Eve too and how happy he would be for us today.)

'So Mum, Mum-in-law, Dad-in-law – please accept these presents as a small token of our thanks. [hand over gifts]

'We'd also like to say a big thank you to my wife's 'best gal' Kath, for all the moral and emotional support, for sorting out these beautiful table decorations, and for a hundred and one other things. Please accept this little thank you... [hand over gift]

'Next, we'd like to say thanks to my best man, Rob, my oldest and blondest friend, who has been a beacon of wisdom and serenity throughout the whole build-up to this day. Thanks Rob for all your friendship and support over the last 36 years... [hand over gift].

'Thanks to my sister Sarah for designing the invitations, and to Cath, Adam, Maria, Jerome, Robbie, Laurence, Hannah and Katie for the musical number.

'We also want to thank Jerry the DJ, Guy the chauffeur, Chris the photographer, Cath the fashion adviser and our readers Paul, Patsy and Marguerite. They've all helped enormously with the day and have been great friends to us both.

'And last but not least, it's only right and proper that we finish on a special note of thanks to the bridesmaids. I think you'll all agree that they look absolutely beautiful, and a special well done to five-year-old Tilly for looking so pretty and holding Eve's dress so patiently.

'So now would you please all stand, raise your glasses and join us in a toast to: "the bridesmaids!"'

Sample speech 2
A touch of the jitters

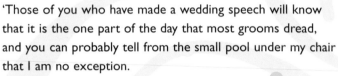

'Those of you who have made a wedding speech will know that it is the one part of the day that most grooms dread, and you can probably tell from the small pool under my chair that I am no exception.

'You may remember that Richard Curtis wrote 17 drafts of *Four Weddings and a Funeral.* Well, I am no Richard Curtis. [pause] I could never be that decisive.

'Actually, of course, the speech I'm really dreading is Jack's (the best man's), because he knows all my secrets. So if you see me slipping out quietly in a few minutes' time, you'll understand why...

'Of course, it's a day that I wouldn't miss for the world, and I have been looking forward to it ever since Fran said she would marry me.

'Footballers say that, in the build-up to a big game, it's the waiting in the tunnel that really makes you nervous. And I have to say that the run-up to the wedding has had an effect on my nerves. Isn't it strange that perfectly normal human beings like me [pause for laughs and heckling] and Fran – mature, adult types who are never lost for words or caught out in a crisis [pause again] – could get so het up about things?

'After all, who really cares if the hotel is double-booked? Who cares if the wedding cake topples over as we try to cut it? Who cares if on the honeymoon... but no, let's not go there.

'And yet, over the last couple of weeks, I've developed some nervous habits, strange abnormal behaviours, which can only be put down to my feelings of apprehension about the forthcoming event.

'On Wednesday I got on a Tube going the wrong way round the Circle Line. Not that it makes much difference on the Circle Line, mind.

'On Thursday, I forgot to set the video for *Countdown*. Worst of all, I've even started getting in on time for work.

'I found myself taking the ring out of its box and looking at it... I wondered: was it too big? Too small? What would happen if I can't get it on Fran's finger? Was it really made of

gold? Was it the right shape? Was it round enough? Crazy questions went round and round in my head.

'I think my beloved might have been suffering a little from wedding jitters too. I was checking my emails the other day, and I found an email from Fran to her best friend Lucy which she had inadvertently copied to me... It said in large capital letters (and I quote): "WHAT AM I DOING? I MUST BE MAD! I'M ONLY 28 AND THAT'S MUCH TOO YOUNG TO COMMIT MYSELF TO A LIFETIME OF WEDLOCK." Which made me think that perhaps Fran wasn't quite so relaxed about the whole thing either.

'So I have a message for Fran, which comes straight from the heart – "I'm just as terrified as you are!" No, no, I mean, don't worry, everything will be all right. With you by my side, I feel ready for anything. I wouldn't have it any other way.

'Now I would just like to say how happy Fran and I are that so many members of the family and friends have been able to come today. It's marvellous to see you all. Unfortunately, the one part of the speech that has managed to survive all the 39 drafts I made is the list of thank yous. And so without further ado...'

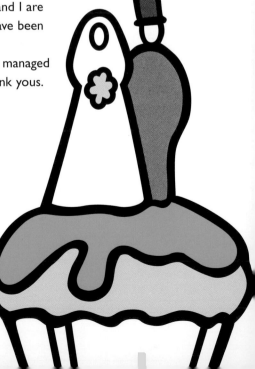

Sample speech 3
Even the best-laid plans...

'First of all, I'd like to thank the staff of the Regent Place Hotel for making us feel so very welcome here. I don't think we realize how much work goes on behind the scenes to make these days a success.

'And, I have to say, that Jo and I may not be the easiest wedding party in the world. Because as some of you will know, we've had a slightly rocky ride over the last few weeks.

'Three weeks ago, everything was going swimmingly. The reception was booked, the cake was ordered, the best man had been duly chosen and primed, and the dress (I was reliably informed) looked gorgeous – not this one, of course – I mean [pretend to squirm] it's just that... what happened was... oh, you'll see in a minute.

'Then we received a phone call from Bali. Jake (the best man) had sprained his ankle scuba diving, and didn't think he was going to make it back in time – any chance I could find a replacement? So I rushed around, priming a few old friends to step into the breach if necessary. Well, as you can see, it wasn't necessary and he did make it back. [Pause for cheers/boos.] Just don't ask him to dance. Or go scuba diving. Or buy a round (well you can try).

'And then there was the dress. Now this is all hearsay, of course, because as per tradition, I was not allowed anywhere near the dress.

'That's right, to my eternal regret, I wasn't allowed to come and sit for hours in the shop while Jo tried on around 262 different dresses. What a shame. I would have enjoyed that. (Luckily the shop had camp beds for Jo and her mum.)

'But I was lucky enough to share in the fraught 3am moment when Jo had a sudden revelation, 48 hours before the big day, that she'd chosen the wrong dress.

'It was touch and go, but thanks to her mum, who stayed up all night making alterations, she finally made it down the aisle in the dress she was happy with. And I'm sure you'll agree with me that the final choice was worth all the kerfuffle. [Pause for cheers.]

'The cake was fairly painless. The only hiccough was when the cake maker (a marvellous lady called Gina who's a friend of Jo's... (Please, everyone, a round of applause for Gina!) rang up one evening when Jo was at the cinema and asked, "Are you planning on a cake with a lot of tiers?"

'I got a bit confused and replied: "Um, no thank you, just the usual ingredients..." Luckily we cleared up the confusion, and you'll be seeing the result in a few moments, and I can assure you, Gina has played an absolute belter...

'But the worst of all was last Wednesday, my stag night. And I promise you this is absolutely a true story. I had organized my do for the Wednesday because I believed that it is not a good idea to have your stag night the evening before the wedding itself. Especially with the friends I've got – chances are that I would now be swimming naked in the sea

off Skegness rather than speaking to you. (Though perhaps some of you would prefer that, who knows?)

'Anyway, myself and a few well-chosen friends, including one on crutches – who found it strangely difficult to get to the bar – were seated in a well-known pub in Hackney, when the mobile rang. This was about 10pm so I was still pretty sober. [pause for boos and heckling]

'It was Jo, and I have to say she was hysterical. And apologetic. Actually considering she was interrupting the second most important event of my life – the first being when United won the treble in 1999 – she wasn't especially apologetic. But she was certainly hysterical.

'She was ringing to say that she had got worried about the reception, and had phoned the Regent Park Hotel just to check if everything was OK for the wedding day. And, of course, the Regent Park Hotel, which I should add is about 23 miles from here on the other side of London, said, "Terribly sorry, madam, we have no record of your booking."

'Eventually I was able to tell her about the Regent Place Hotel, where we'd actually planned to have the reception, and put her mind at rest. But in all the confusion, time had ticked by, and it was gone last orders. So for this reason we were obliged to find somewhere else to have one last drink. So really it was my wife's fault that we got stuck in Stringfellows all that time...

''So you see, we've had a few blips along the way. I mentioned this to Jo's mum Teresa just now, as we were waiting for Jo to get to the church. (Well, I had to pass the time somehow.) And Teresa told me that when she got married, the Rolls-Royce taking her away from the church got a puncture in Ealing High Road, and she had to walk the rest of the way to the reception.

It's a funny thing, isn't it, that you try your best to make sure everything goes without a hitch, but then it's the things that go wrong that make the day so memorable? And, of course, it doesn't really matter if things go a bit awry, because – as I now know – this day will be the happiest of my life.

'Now, finally, I'd like to take this opportunity to thank a whole host of people for making today such a success...'

Sample speech 4
Here at last!

'It's wonderful and a little bit strange to be standing in front of you today. Wonderful, because Marcia and I are actually getting married, and I can see dozens of faces of family and friends who have been kind enough to come here today.

'Strange, because, as some of you will know, it has taken Marcia and me a little while to actually arrive at this day.

'In fact, I proposed to Marcia on 4 June 2002 – no less than four years, six months and 32 days ago. Now I have been on to the *Guinness Book of Records*, and they tell me that the longest ever engagement was 84 years and nine months, so there's no chance of us getting in the book. (Though I've a hunch we're in the Top Ten...)

'Now all of you will know that Marcia and I are pretty decisive people [pause for laughs/ironic cheers] and I wouldn't like you to think that we have been having doubts about the wedding. Not at all. You may remember that the reason I proposed on 4 June 2002 was because on 5 June 2002, Marcia decided to leave for Dubai for two years. It seemed like a good idea at the time...

'Then, when Marcia came back from Dubai, it took a while for us to get back into the rhythm of the relationship, so to speak. Actually it took three weeks just to get all the sand out of her clothes.

'Marcia had been living in an all-female compound, so she wasn't used to having a man around. Living together after all that time was hard work, there were tears, tantrums, irrational outbursts. And that was just me.

'However, I can tell you now that never at any time did I doubt that eventually Marcia and I would be walking up the aisle of the church as we did today. Well, once perhaps. One day I came in from work and found Marcia dancing around the flat with very little on. [pause for cheers etc.] That in itself was not a problem. It was the fact that she was singing *You're Beautiful* by James Blunt that was the worry. He's very popular in Dubai, apparently.

'But in my heart I knew that nothing would stop me from marrying Marcia. It was just a question of time. Quite a long time as it turned out, because a couple of months after that, I was posted to HMS *Gordon* in Scapa Flow.

'I think Marcia was frustrated by my accepting this posting, but when the Navy says "Jump!", you jump. I couldn't imagine myself going to the First Lord of the Admiralty saying "I'm sorry, my Lord, but Marcia's getting impatient for the big day."

'But anyway, two years later and we are all here. Better late than never. Perhaps better late than early, too, because if you have to wait and wait for something, then when it finally arrives, you appreciate it all the more. Remember Christmas morning, opening your presents? You've waited for it for weeks and finally it's here. Well, that's how it feels now. Marcia, my love, you are worth the wait.

'One advantage of our prolonged engagement is that I've had plenty of time to write my speech. Really? I hear you say, we wouldn't have noticed. But my speech is really a chance to thank lots of people who have made the day such a success. And so let me begin by thanking...'

Sample speech 5
Age difference?

'Looking around me today, I can see a lot of familiar faces – family and friends from all the parts of my life, which is marvellous. But I can also see some less familiar faces as well – and that is good too because it means that there are still more friends to be made once the speeches are over. Doubtless you are all looking forward to that moment almost as much as me...

'Some of you on my side may not be very familiar with Emma and vice versa, so let me give you a bit of background. Emma and I met about three years ago when we were both giving papers at a conference in Cologne. In fact I literally bumped into her in the bar, when she turned round and swept the tray of drinks I was holding on to the floor.

'What I remember most clearly was that she didn't say sorry. She just said "Oh!" Just that: "Oh!" Never apologize, never explain! Oh yes, I shall always remember that distinctive "Oh!" de Cologne... [pause for laughs/groans]

'Now, you may have noticed that there is something of an age difference between us. Emma is young and beautiful, whereas I am older and... comfortable. In fact, at that conference in Cologne, she was the youngest speaker, and I was the second oldest.

'The more traditionally minded among you may tut at this. But let me just point out that the age difference between Emma and me is exactly half that between Bruce Forsyth and *Strictly Come Dancing* co-host Tess Daley. And when you see the pair of us gliding across the dance floor later on...

'In fact, Emma is 24 years and 6 months younger than me. Since she doesn't look a day over 16, and I do look a day over my actual age, the only surprise you're probably registering at the moment is that the gap is not actually greater.

'It means, as those of you with good memories will already have worked out, that in the year that Emma was born, I had already graduated from Hull University, started and been sacked from my first job.

'And Margaret Thatcher had not yet taken on Arthur Scargill. (By the way, for the younger ones: Margaret Thatcher was Prime Minister in the 1980s and Arthur Scargill was... just let me remember... it'll come in a minute... [shake head despairingly] No, it's gone. My memory's not so good these days...)

'Some people will say that when my wife – what a nice expression that is, let me just try it again: "MY WIFE!!!"...is 50, I shall already be an old man. They may even suggest that we'll need to employ someone younger to inject some vim and vigour into the relationship. I thank those people for their concern, but let me reassure you all: one youthful partner will be more than enough for me!

'For her part, Emma says she is perfectly happy with the arrangement. As a way of reassuring me (and perhaps herself?!) she's been keeping a list of famous older fathers: John Simpson, war correspondent; John Humphrys, presenter of the *Today* programme on Radio 4; Luciano Pavarotti, ex-opera singer. Not a bad list so far... and it just gets better: Rod Stewart, Paul McCartney, Stevie Wonder, Brad Pitt...

'Brad Pitt? I leave it to the guests to decide which one I most resemble.

'At the end of the day, I hope you'll agree with me that it doesn't matter one hoot. Because, you see, like all older and... comfortable people, I feel completely young at heart. And in any case, when I met Emma, it never occurred to me to think of her as being 26 or 43 or 165... she was just Emma.

'Now, I am sure you lot are keen to get dancing and canoodling and [put on doddery old man's voice] all those things that you young people like to do. But before this old man collapses in front of you, I have a few people that I really want to thank for making today such a success...'

Sample speech 6
In sickness and in health

'My wife and I [pause for cheering] would like to thank everyone for being here today. Now I know you're all keen for me to get my bit over with so you can hear what my best man has to say about my embarrasssing youth, adolescence and adult life. Before that, though, I feel I have to share with you a couple of uncanny events leading up to today.

'You may have noticed the cast that John, my best man is sporting today. No, we didn't have a last minute fight about the content of his speech, the stag night or my suitability for married life – had that been the case I'm sure it'd be me on crutches. Or worse; John's a karate black belt.

'Admittedly, I was there when John broke his leg, but I held the ladder he was climbing to clean out the gutter really steady, honest! If only I'd insisted on carrying the ladder back to the garage to put it away. Yes, believe it or not, it was on the 'hazardous' walk across the lawn that disaster struck – John slipped on some leaves and managed to fracture his tibia. (For those that aren't medically minded that's a bone between your knee and your ankle.) I'd never been to the casualty department of St Thomas's before, but when this all happened the Saturday before last, I definitely remember thinking to myself, "Must remember where it is in case I ever need to go again".

'Obviously, I didn't expect to be going back there anytime soon, if ever. How wrong I was. Last Saturday I decided I'd better try to give Amy a hand with all the preparations for today [pause for heckling]. She was about to start cutting out the fabric to make the bridal favours on your tables. "I know," I said, "Why don't I pop over to my Mum and Dad's and borrow Mum's circular cutter for you – it'll be easier won't it?" For those of you that don't know, a circular cutter is like a pizza wheel, but much, MUCH sharper.

'Unfortunately, though warned by my Mum, I failed to take on board just how sharp this piece of equipment is. As I was handing it to Amy, my hand slipped, and you can all imagine what happened next. Amy quickly realized that the cut to my hand needed a couple of stitches. So there I was, in casualty for the second Saturday in a row. The staff even recognized me! With this in mind, my first thank you is to the wonderful staff at St Thomas's.'

[Continue speech with the rest of the thanks.]

Sample speech 7
Fear of speeches

'Today has been a terrifying day. When I woke up this morning, I was terrified because in a few short hours, I would be getting married. Now of course I am ecstatic to be married to a wonderful woman like Carol, but getting married is a pretty big thing, and like all big things, a little bit terrifying.

'Mind you, tying the knot and committing myself to spending the rest of my life with Carol is nothing compared to my very real fear of what my best man Dave is going to reveal about me in his speech.

'The thought of him standing in front of you all and telling you some of the things we have got up to over the past ten years is truly daunting. But before he speaks, please bear this in mind: any incidents he mentions – and don't let him persuade you otherwise – were always, always his idea.

'Dave, if you do right by me, I'll promise not to mention the Affair of the Purple Pants in the Chicken Korma. Do we have a deal?

'Still, if getting married and having the person who knows you best and who has been present at the scene of your worst excesses making a speech about you in front of your nearest and dearest isn't terrifying enough, there is one final, terrifying ordeal left before I can sit down and really start to enjoy married life.

'I'm talking, of course, about making this speech. Some people love the sound of their own voices – Dave, for instance – and some of us are a bit more reticent. Speaking personally, even when I'm in a small group and someone suggests that we all "go round and say a few words by way of introduction", I forget my own name and am reduced to a mound of shivering jelly.

'So the thought of having to stand in front of you today and make a speech, as I'm doing right now, is perhaps a large part of the reason why Carol and I spent over five years being engaged without actually getting married. That's my story anyway – I'm still not sure what Carol's excuse is...

'When I confided my fear, people always said to me: 'You'll be alright; just be yourself'. But what if yourself is a gibbering wreck whose tongue has stuck to the floor of his mouth?

'Now I consider myself a pretty rational sort of fellow [pause for howls of disagreement]. I cheerfully walk under ladders, I break mirrors with impunity and I've even been known to say "Macbeth" in the middle of am-dram productions.

'So I understand that my fear of making speeches is actually a pretty irrational one. It's even got a fancy psychiatric name: "glossophobia". That sounds like it should be fear of lip gloss, and funnily enough I do also have that fear. (Although this probably doesn't count as irrational when you have been accosted as many times as I have by a drunk and very dribbly, wet-lipped Dave muttering "You're my best mate, I really love you man..." before passing out on your carpet.)

'Anyway, I was desperate to kick this problem because I didn't want this silly phobia of mine to stand in the way of marrying the love of my life. I decided that it was high time to 'feel my fear and do it anyway', to give my glossophobia the elbow.

'Someone told me that hypnosis was a great way to sort the problem. I was terrified that I'd be put in a trance and made to shout "I'm a pink pixie!" whenever I heard a certain noise forever afterwards. But a colleague who'd tried something similar said it had really helped him, so I swallowed my anxiety and headed off to a hypnotherapy workshop...

'It all started well enough with coffee and biscuits while we waited for everyone to arrive, then the hypnotherapist suggested we take it in turns to stand up and introduce ourselves and say what it was that we hoped hypnotherapy would achieve and.... Well you can imagine the rest.

'Anyway, I stuck with it for a few sessions and I am now delighted to say that whatever the hypnotherapist did seems to have worked, because here I am now in front of my wonderful new wife, my family, Carol's family, and my wonderful, wonderful friends, making a speech without fear. Well, not without fear, but at least some intelligible sound is coming out of my mouth, which is a major improvement.

'I stand before you a married man, ready for whatever Dave "Purple Pants" Williams wants to throw at me – and I have almost reached the end of my speech without passing out. What can I add except that in marrying Carol I consider myself to be the happiest and most fortunate man alive. And I know I speak for both of us when I say how delighted we are that you are all here to share this special moment with us...

[At this point, as pre-arranged, a member of the wedding party sounds a horn or rings a bell. Shout out in a funny squeaky voice:] 'I'M A PINK PIXIE!!'

[Now carry on as normal with the rest of the speech.] And so to the thank yous...

Sample speech 8

A night to remember

'I have to say that whoever it was who invented weddings and the protocol that goes with them was an absolute genius.

'That's because as the groom I get to make my speech before the best man's, which means I can steal his thunder and get in with my version of the stag night before he gives you his.

'As you listen to the two accounts that follow of that memorable night, you'll probably notice some key differences, and you'll have to decide who you think is the most reliable witness. It'll be my word against his. And please remember: it's my day, so you're supposed to be on my side... [pause, then pleading:] Please.

'Of course, the point of a stag night is to have one final, irresponsible night of wild abandon before settling in to married life. It's a profound event in a young man's life which signals the end of one era and the beginning of another.

'It's the end of going out every night and getting stupidly drunk, having a ridiculously hot curry and falling asleep in front of the telly, waking up at two in the morning with a mouth like the inside of a budgie's cage.

'Thank God I don't have to do that any more.

'More important, it's the start of the rest of my life, a life which I get to share with my beautiful new wife. Plus, I'll never have to cook again! Only joking... I'm always happy to lend a hand at barbecue time.

'Now as you'd all agree, any important ritual must be performed correctly – in accordance with ancient custom – if it's to have its full meaning and spiritual value. When it comes to the stag night, venerable custom dictates that a shaman – a master of ceremonies, a high priest of high living – be on hand to administer the ritual and ensure that no details, however small, are overlooked.

'This person is known as the best man, though I would have thought that 'sadistic sod who makes you drink far too much and takes you to places you'd rather not even talk about' would be far more appropriate.

'In other words, Gavin here was the perfect man for the job, and he carried out his sacred duty above and beyond the call of even the most fundamentalist fanatic.

'The stag night he organized for me was extreme, cruel and unusual, and Gavin, old son, I wouldn't have had it any other way.

'So what did we get up to? I think it's fair to say that some things are much better left unsaid, and many of the details of that night definitely fall into that category, especially since my parents and young children are present. I, for one, will never be able to look a traffic warden in the face again.

'What I can tell you is that Gavin and his associates made me drink a great deal of lager. At least, they told me it was lager. It was oddly green for lager, the colour in fact of crème de menthe.

'I remember too that Gavin had reminded my fellow revellers of my childhood obsession with Marmite, and thought it'd be a good idea to spread this news about. Literally. All over me.

'I can't quite recall all the details after that but I do remember that at one point Gavin appeared to be taking a fancy to a young lady, who wanted his name and address. That, Gavin, is because she was a policewoman.

'Fortunately she had a sense of humour, and let Gavin go with a warning when she realized that he was only carrying out his sacred, time-honoured duty.

'Perhaps the best way to sum up the evening is to summarize Gavin's state the next morning. There he lay, pale as a very pale thing, nursing the mother of all hangovers, moaning gently and swearing he was never going to drink

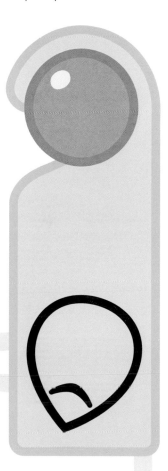

another drop again, and that if I ever saw him with an alcoholic drink in his hand I should shoot him.

'I have to say that I was truly touched to see him in such a state: to think he had done all that to himself just for me. Gav, you've been a fantastic friend over the years, and you acquitted yourself in your duties admirably.

'All I can say is that I am fantastically glad I don't have to go through that again, and delighted that from now on it won't be the sight of you, hungover and smelly, lying on my sofa, that I have to wake up to. It will be my beautiful bride instead.

'Oddly you seem to have forgotten that your own stag do is only six months or so away, and that I have the honour of being your best man on that occasion.

'So as I stand here on this auspicious day before all my loved ones, let me make this solemn oath to you: [put hand on heart] "Gav, I hereby promise before everyone present that I shall strive with every sinew of my being to carry out my best-man duties with the same enthusiasm and rigour that you brought to the job. Amen."'

Sample speech 9
Why get married?

'The song says: "Love and marriage go together like a horse and carriage". Well, nowadays, you don't see many horses and carriages on the road, and when you do people stare, and you end up with a traffic jam. So perhaps it's not surprising that many people these days wonder what exactly the point of getting married is.

'In fact, when we announced we were going to tie the knot, some of you expressed surprise that such forward-looking and free-thinking people as us [pause] should want to take such an apparently old-fashioned step.

'So let me explain why we decided to take the plunge.

'Don't worry – we're not going to get all religious on you. It wasn't about religion. Nor was our decision to tie the knot taken to fit in with anyone else's opinions about what relationships should be. We didn't choose to get married because other people wanted us to, however much we love you all. No, we chose to get married because it was what we wanted.

'As you all know, we've been together for a number of years now. At first, we were on a bit of a learning curve getting to know each other better. But then when we'd been a couple for a while and we'd spent a few holidays together without actually killing each other, we decided to take it one step further and move in together.

'When we told our families, there were various reactions. Some of my mates were a bit upset at the thought that there might be fewer nights out with the lads. But I hope they can now see that, even if I am a bit less available for nights at the pub, I'm a better friend to them because of the strength I get from Sarah.

'And Sarah, of course, is perfectly capable of drinking most of them under the table anyway.

'Sarah's Auntie Mabel, meanwhile (God rest her soul) announced that we were embarking on the road for Hell. Well, I hope she can see from where she is now that we are not any worse as people after four years of 'living in sin'.

'Of course, for some people, life under the same roof turns out to be hell on earth. But for us there wasn't even a hint of purgatory. I can honestly say that we've been happy together from day one. Even the rows we've had have ended up with us feeling closer (perhaps it's the making up afterwards) and we've never doubted our future together.

'And that brings me to the heart of what I have to say. We were happy as a couple before today's ceremony, and we don't think our life will be very different after it. So why did we do it, I hear you ask? For the sake of the children we hope to have? For the tax and financial advantages? Of course not.

'No – the real reason is quite simply the best one: because we feel so lucky, so blessed, to have found one another that we want to celebrate that love with all of you today. We wanted to say thank you to all our loved ones – family and friends – who have contributed to our happiness. To share this happiest of times with the people who mean most to us.

'Now I've a long list of thank yous to make, but let me begin with this one. Thank you all for coming to celebrate with us the love which unites us and has made us so happy. Thank you for all your love and support so far – and please continue to be there for us as we will always be for you.

[insert thank you section]

'Ladies and gentlemen, I'd like to give you a toast: to love and marriage!'

Sample speech 10
My new family

'In thanking my new parents-in-law Jane and Bernard tonight, I'm not just being polite and following wedding etiquette. From the first moment I met them they accepted me wholeheartedly and put me at ease with effortless and sincere kindness. Thank you, Jane and Bernard, for trusting me with your beautiful daughter.

'You've all heard the corny old line about not losing a daughter but gaining a son. Well in fact, neither of them has ever given the impression that they thought I was taking Liz away from them. From the first they accepted me as part of the family. I don't know if they see me as a son. But they have become something else which I treasure: real friends.

'I remember the first time I met them as if it were yesterday. Terrifying! Seeing *Meet the Parents* the night before was probably a bad idea. Everyone knows the scene where the hapless fiancé makes gaffe after gaffe at his first dinner with his in-laws, even managing to smash an urn containing his fiancée's granny's ashes.

'Well, things didn't get that bad but I certainly was nervous. Liz obviously adored her parents and I was terrified that I wouldn't measure up. But very quickly, the evening turned from a frightening obligation into really good fun.

'The food was fantastic – thanks Jane. The wine was even better – thanks Bernard. And Bernard's jokes were... well, you can't have everything.

'We all like to think we're our own people, completely self-made, but of course we're all products of our upbringing too. It was when I met Liz's parents that I realized where she got so many of the qualities I admire in her: her tolerance, her unflappable nature, her keen interest in people and the world around her.

'It was Jane and Bernard, she told me, who taught her to try new things and tolerate people's differences. So it's thanks to them that she not only puts up with hours of football on the TV, but has even learned to show (or should that be 'feign'?) an interest in it.

'But tolerance has its limits, she says, and she still can't stand darts. So, Bernard, you still have one or two things to teach her before your work is done...

'Of course, Liz hasn't inherited all her parents' talents. She would be the first to admit that she's a stranger to the kitchen so it's lucky I can

cook a bit – and that there's a great Indian takeaway next door! Perhaps the perfection of Bernard's garden is the reason why she has never picked up a hoe or a pair of secateurs.

'Well, I guess it's just as well that we live on the third floor.

'Are there any qualities she has which they don't? I'm getting onto dangerous ground here, I know, and I don't want to ruin the start of a beautiful friendship by putting my foot in it tonight. Maybe I could just mention one thing, though.

'I have already mentioned Jane and Bernard's unflappable nature. They are both very calm, self-controlled people, so I can't imagine that their influence is behind the way Liz demonstrates her newfound enthusiasm for football. I can't see Jane or Bernard screaming the house down when England miss a penalty! Liz has become a true fan – maybe that one's down to me!

'Jane and Bernard, thank you again for trusting me to make your daughter happy. I will give my all to try to be faithful to that trust. But above all, thank you for making her the wonderful person she is, the person who today is the reason for making me so happy.'

Sample speech 11
My beautiful bride

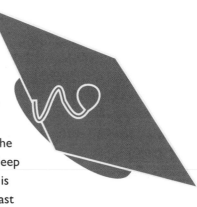

'Having thanked all those who contributed to today's celebration, I now come to the most important thank you of all. I want to say thank you to my beautiful new wife for saying "I do".

'Of course, you all know I have to say that Suzanne is the most beautiful woman in the world. Otherwise I have to sleep on the sofa tonight. But in fact she really, really is. Suzanne is beautiful, kind and intelligent – although you may find the last bit hard to believe, since she chose me!

'As you all know, Suzanne has many wonderful attributes. There are lots of sides to her I could talk about, without ever tiring. Each of you will have your favourite: the successful career woman, the brilliant cook, the generous and faithful friend.

'But my favourite of all has to be her sense of humour. (Now I can hear you all thinking: "Ah! So that's why she chose you!")

'When we met I was terrified – I'd spotted this gorgeous girl across the room at a party, but I didn't dare approach her. She was surrounded by smart and attractive guys all evening, and I didn't think I'd get a look in.

'After an hour or two I confided to our host the reasons for my despondency, and he took pity on me and introduced us. (Thank you Mike, by the way. He's here tonight, folks. Please give him a big hand, for making not just my evening but my whole life!) I was so nervous I couldn't get the conversation going properly, but it didn't take Suzanne long to break the ice.

'Suzanne just kept making jokes. At first I was laughing out of nervousness but by the end of the evening we were both giggling like idiots – and not just out of pity on Suzanne's part, I hope. Darling, the smile you put on my face that night has been there ever since, and I think it'll stay there as long as I live.

'Suzanne later told me that it was my shyness that had attracted her most that night. Apparently the other guys around her were all a bit full of themselves, trying too hard to impress. After all those show-offs, she said she found me refreshingly natural and modest.

'No really!

'I can already hear my friends sniggering. Some of them, it seems, think I am not quite as shy and modest as I am making out. Well, Suzanne is the brains in our relationship (and the beauty, too) so I'll happily abide by her judgement.

'But seriously, folks... As I got to know Suzanne I very quickly realized that at last I had found someone that I didn't have to put on an act for, someone who accepted me exactly as I am, warts and all (no comments, please!). So let me give a word of advice to those of you still looking for your other half: just be yourselves, don't show off, and with a bit of luck you might just land on your feet as spectacularly as I have!

'Well, the clock is ticking and I can see some eyes glazing over and others looking wistfully at the glass in front of them. I promised Suzanne I wouldn't go on too long so I'd better wind up if I don't want to be on the receiving end of one of her famous put-downs!

'So let me begin our thank yous by thanking again the lovely wife who has made me happier today than I ever thought it possible to be.'

Sample speech 12
Sweet and loving

'As Jane Austen said "It is a truth universally acknowledged that a single man in possession of a good fortune must be in want of a wife."

'Now much as I like to think I am Mr Darcy, and that only bouncing a few cheques to the florist for today establishes me as a man of good fortune, my real good fortune in life is undoubtedly meeting, and marrying my wife, Chloe.

'She certainly, as somebody else said, has a price beyond rubies, and I'd like to thank my new father-in-law for his kind words and his making me the richest man in the world by letting me marry her.

'You have all helped make today the happiest day of our lives by being here with us and being kind enough to bring gifts. I never knew that toasters came in so many varieties! Seriously, the greatest gift to us is your being here, and I hope that you enjoy the day half as much as we are.

'My wife (I love saying that!) would not be the person she is without the love and support of her parents, and I want to thank them for helping her to be her and for welcoming me into their family. As my new mother-in-law said, she is not losing a daughter but gaining a washer-upper. While not quite so useful, I hope that she will accept this small gift as a sign of how much I appreciate her love and support, especially through the nerve-wracking preparations for the wedding.

'All that hard work was worth it. Sarah looks even more beautiful than she does normally, and I hope that I will be everything she could ever hope for in a husband. If there is one thing I have learnt from her, it is patience, and today was worth all the waiting.

'Sarah, I just want to say, in front of our families and dearest friends, that I love you and hope that every day will be as happy as today – just not as expensive.

'Not only did Bob, my old roommate from Uni days and the best man I know, get me to the church on time but he also didn't lose the ring. I'm grateful for everything that he's done for me and look forward to returning the compliment – as soon as possible.

'Lastly, I would like to thank the pack of bridesmaids, who have been such good friends throughout all the preparations. In particular, I would like to thank Vikki, the chief bridesmaid, who has been there every step of the way, from the wedding dress shop to the hairdressers, offering advice and support, even if it was only to mutter something about looking like a meringue! Please accept these flowers in thanks for everything you've done.

'Ladies and gentlemen, please be upstanding. I give you... the bridesmaids.'

Sample speech 13
Short and sweet

'Having listened to such words of wisdom from my new father-in-law, I can only hope that I am worthy of them. Thank you, Ken.

I''m really pleased that you could all make it here today, but I'm especially grateful to the Johnsons, who've travelled all the way from Edinburgh to be with us. I knew that it was worth including the words "free bar" on the invitations!

'You've all been very generous, not only by being here today to share this happy occasion, but also by giving us so many wonderful gifts.

'My parents brought me up to believe that good things come to those who wait, and I want to thank them for being right and for being there whenever I needed them, especially this morning when Dad helped me do up my tie as I was shaking so much. Thanks, both of you.

'I now have a new set of parents, the in-laws. Contrary to all the horror stories, mine are amazing, but I always knew that they would be, as no one could raise so perfect a woman as my wife if they weren't wonderful themselves. I want to thank them for helping us to have the best wedding we could ever have dreamed of. Thank you, Ken and Angela, for your kindness and for raising such a beautiful daughter.

'Sarah, no one could have made me as happy as you have these last few years, and I look forward to growing old and grey with you.

'And going grey is something that almost happened prematurely when we were on the way to the church and Bob realized that he'd left the ring behind. Fortunately, everything else went according to plan, and it was great to have my best man at my side.

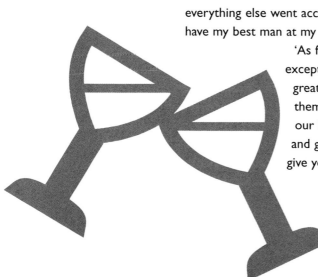

'As for the bridesmaids, what can I say except they look lovely and have been great through all the preparations? I'd like them to accept these small offerings with our love. They deserve a drink so, ladies and gentlemen, please be upstanding. I give you... the bridesmaids.'

Sample speech 14
Second marriages

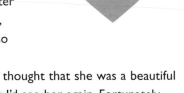

'This is a second marriage for both of us, and I am grateful for the words my new father-in-law has just spoken. Sarah and I feel privileged to have found each other and to be given a second chance of love.

'My parents have been particularly supportive over the last few weeks when wedding nerves set in, but this was to be expected as they've always been there for me, no matter what. I know that Sarah feels the same about her parents, who have welcomed me into their family and have been so generous, helping us with this wedding.

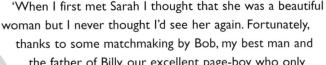

'When I first met Sarah I thought that she was a beautiful woman but I never thought I'd see her again. Fortunately, thanks to some matchmaking by Bob, my best man and the father of Billy, our excellent page-boy who only tried to eat the cushion once, we did see each other again. I'd like to thank him for helping us get where we are today. Sarah and I will always be grateful for his interference!

'Sarah believes strongly that looks are less important than personality, which is just as well, otherwise she wouldn't have agreed to marry me! Sarah has taught me the importance of patience and compromise as our families have united to make a whole, and I am grateful to her that she has helped me make this transition quite so easily. Standing here today, in front of you all, I have to say that it has definitely been worth it.

'Obviously our wedding would be nothing without the love and blessing of our children: Claire, David and Simon. Claire has told me confidentially, so you'll have to keep this to yourselves, that she's always wanted a brother. So now that she's got two, I hope that she'll be twice as happy. David and Simon, I'd like to say how delighted I am to be your step-father. And Claire, Sarah has asked me to say that you are the daughter she thought she would never have.

'Sarah's sister, Vikki, has been a tower of strength through all the pre-wedding stress. So for that and for your fantastic flower arrangements, thank you, Vikki. And for those of you who are wondering how we spent the money that we saved on the flowers, we spent it on extra booze! So, take advantage and raise your glasses to... Bob and Vikki.'

How to include children of a previous marriage

- I've always been terribly grateful to Sarah's children, Fiona and Jack. Sarah's experience raising them has surely made her more prepared to take me on, although I do promise to clean my room and do my homework from now on.
- I'm delighted that my sons John and Peter and Sasha's daughter Melanie are here to share today – and the rest of our lives – with us. They're wonderful people.
- I count myself doubly lucky that the young lady over there, Tina, Geraldine's daughter, can be with us today. It is a delight and a privilege to know her, and thank you, Tina, for all the help you've given us preparing for this wedding.

Sample speech 15

Personal and humorous

'That was a hard act to follow. I hope I'll be able to look after Felicity as well as you have, Dick.

'Thank you all for coming here today, especially everyone who has travelled from the other side of the Atlantic to share this day with us. May I just let you all know we think Guildford is quite a large town around here, so please stop referring to it as 'cute' and 'quaint' and saying how nice it would look in the back yard.

'Thank you also for your generous gifts. We're actually a bit upset, as we threw out our old toaster yesterday in anticipation of receiving several more. We've opened most of the gifts and no one seems to have given us one.

'Of course, none of us would be here today without Felicity's parents – Shirley and Dick – and my parents – Flora and Johnny. When I met Felicity, I thought she was sincere, kind and caring, and when I met her parents, I knew exactly where she got it from. It's clearly genetic, and I hope our children will inherit it.

'Flora and Johnny have been so supportive to me – always. I've worried sometimes that I'm not good enough for Felicity, but my mum has always assured me I am. And even though I know she's biased, I was egotistical enough to believe her, and here I am today. So, Shirley and Flora, we'd like to give you these little tokens of our love and thanks.

'My love and thanks today really have to go to Felicity – for being here, for being so beautiful and for being my wife.

As an investment banker, Felicity deals with mergers and acquisitions. On this occasion, I'm thrilled she's mixed business with pleasure and merged with my family and acquired me!

'You've all met Aloysius, my best man. When I asked him to be best man, I checked with him that he could organize a stag night, make a speech, even get me to the church on time. But I forgot to ask the most important thing: could he tie the knot? I'm not talking about marriage here, I'm talking about the horrendous mess he's made of my bow tie!

'Thank you also to the beautiful bridesmaids. I know they and Oddbins have been a great support to Felicity during the last few months. Felicity, Laura, Sarah, Johanna and Chardonnay met up so often I was confused as to why there are only three bridesmaids here today.

'Ladies and gentlemen, Chardonnay could not be with us today, but Champagne has kindly stepped into the breach, so if you would all raise your glasses. I give you... the bridesmaids!'

Toasts

Raise your glass! Making toasts

Today's increasingly sophisticated wedding speeches have evolved from traditional toasts where guests drank the health of the newlyweds. And although toasts are now often only one element of a larger speech, they still have an important role to play. Today there are likely to be several toasts given throughout the day to and by various members of the wedding party.

At larger, more formal occasions, toasts provide a natural break in the proceedings that everyone can recognize. And, at smaller, more informal weddings, a beautiful sentiment expressed in a simple toast that comes from the heart can be as emotionally charged as a full-on speech. Here we offer advice on making a top toast, together with plenty of sample toasts you can adapt for your own use.

What are toasts for?

Toasts can help to punctuate a always hectic and complicated day by alerting guests to the end of speeches, and to the transition from one part of the wedding day to the next.

Toasts should have a clear purpose, whether it's simply to salute the bride and groom (usually the job of the best man) or to honour friends and family who couldn't make it and/or who have passed away.

Toasts can also serve as a natural break in the proceedings if you have gone through a long list of thank-yous or other messages. And they're a quick and easy way to express additional thanks to specific members of the wedding party, such as the bridesmaids. When you are presenting gifts during a toast, for instance to your mother, the bride's mother or the bridesmaids, make sure you leave time for the exchange to take place.

Classic groom's toasts

Traditionally, the groom toasts the bridesmaids/maid of honour. You may also choose to toast your wife, who will then reply and toast the bridesmaids. You may also toast the hosts – traditionally your new in-laws, especially if there are no bridesmaids.

For the in-laws

'Apparently, I'm now supposed to toast our hosts, my parents-in-law. That's a bit of a shame because I think I'd rather have them spit-roasted with onions and lots of garlic. Oh, that kind of toast. Awfully sorry, Mr and Mrs Johnson: you know I think you're good enough to eat! To Mr and Mrs Johnson, ladies and gentlemen!'

To be upstanding...

'And so, without further ado, let me ask those of you who still can, to stand up and join me in a toast...'

'And so will everyone now please raise their glasses – and themselves...'

'I'd like to propose a toast to the most beautiful young ladies in the room – apart from my wife, of course – my mother-in-law and my mother!'

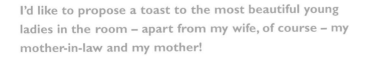

For the parents

'A wedding is a coming together of two families, and I couldn't have wished to join a friendlier family than Stella's, so I'd like to end my speech by thanking our hosts and my new parents-in-law, Betty and Stan, for making this such a wonderful occasion. It's often said that wedding days belong to the happy couple, but there are many people who have helped to make today so perfect. I'd also like to thank my parents, Pauline and Max, for everything they've done for us. Without the hard work of our parents, Stella and I wouldn't have been able to concentrate on having such a good time today! Please raise your glasses to them.'

For the grandparents

'Here's to the few who made this crew. To the grandparents!'

'To the greatest grandparents. I've got a feeling that you might be great-grandparents very soon!'

'I'd like to end my speech by toasting our grandparents We owe them everything: without them we simply wouldn't be here today!'

For the bride

'I'd like to end my speech by proposing a toast to my bride. Without wishing to embarrass anyone by getting too sentimental, Charlotte is all I have ever dreamed of. Someone once said that to love is to receive a glimpse of heaven. Well, I feel I am truly in heaven today... Please raise your glasses to the beautiful bride.'

'I'd like you all to fill your glasses and toast Mary, my bride and joy!'

'With every passing day that I've known you, you've got more and more beautiful. But looking at you today, my darling, you already look like tomorrow.'

'Here's to you and here's to me. Let's hope we never disagree. Here's to our families and our honoured guests. And here's to you never wearing those horrid string vests.'

'Please be upstanding for a toast to my beautiful wife. Helen, we drink today to you – to your charm, your warmth, your sense of humour and your beauty. I hope to give you everything you need to make you happy for the rest of our lives.'

'I'd like to end my speech by toasting my wife: Anna, I hope you remain as happy for the rest of your life as I feel today. To Anna!'

For the bridesmaids

'I'd like to take this opportunity to thank the bridesmaids for their sterling work. I've discovered that for an occasion like this, you really do need to have experts on table flowers, leg-waxing, eyelash-curling and themed party favours on hand, and Alice, Hannah and Ellen certainly fit the bill. They really have been essential in making this a perfect day. Ladies and gentlemen, please raise your glasses to the bridesmaids.'

'I always thought that bridesmaids wore salmon pink dresses with big puffy sleeves and huge bows at the rear. Apparently the shops just don't stock dresses like that any more, so sorry to disappoint you all. However, I'm sure you'll all agree that Jess, Clare and Sandra look gorgeous today. Thank you for all your help – to the bridesmaids!'

'Jane, I've never seen you looking so beautiful. And Jess, Clare and Sandra, you've scrubbed up pretty well, too. Ladies and gentlemen, please raise your glasses to my absolutely stunning wife and her almost-as-stunning bridesmaids. The bride and bridesmaids!'

'Three bridesmaids but only one best man! Now, before there's any fighting, I think I'd better warn you ladies that Owen has two left feet and may possibly tread on your toes. Apart from the considerable pain this may cause, I'm told that you may be more put off by the fact that he could ruin those lovely shoes you're all wearing... Ladies and gentlemen, please raise your glasses to the bridesmaids and their shoes!'

'I'd like to end my speech with a few words about the matron of honour, Alice. Initially Jane asked Alice to be one of her 'bridesmaids'. But as you can see from Alice's beautiful baby bump, the term 'bridesmaid' wouldn't have quite suited her today! Alice, we'd both like to thank you for all your help over the past few months, and we're extremely relieved there's a logical explanation for you suddenly not feeling up to going dress shopping, having to nip to the ladies in every single department store, and not being able to face a post-shopping glass of wine. So, please raise your glasses to Alice and her beautiful bump!'

'Although we don't have any bridesmaids as such, Emma's best friend Corrine has been invaluable in her help and support. So please raise your glasses to Corrine!'

'I'd like to end by proposing a toast to our lovely daughter Rachel – who is also of course our bridesmaid!'

'Please raise your glasses to my sister Jane – our chief bridesmaid. I didn't notice how beautiful she was until today!'

'There's an old saying about always being the bridesmaid and never the bride. Well, I'm very pleased that I've finally made Jane my bride. She's been bridesmald for two of her bridesmaids, and I think she was beginning to worry that the old saying would be true! Please raise your glasses in a toast to my gorgeous bride and her lovely bridesmaids.'

For everybody

'Traditionally, the final part of my speech is to raise a toast to
the bridesmaids, but I'd like to do more than that. In a break
from tradition, both Jane and I would like to propose a toast
to everyone who has helped make the day special – which
includes the bridesmaids, ushers, best man, our parents and
every single one of you for being here. So, to everybody!'

For absent friends

'As most of you know, Debbie's Mum, Janet passed away
last year and so can't be with us today. Judging by the
beautiful weather though, and the fact that everything
(so far at least!) has gone according to plan and pretty
much on time, we think she's probably lending a helping
hand from above. So please raise your glasses to Janet!'

'I'd like to propose a toast to Lorraine's sister Amelia, who
would have been here as a bridesmaid today, but gave birth
to her first baby, a boy called Edward, just two days ago! To
Amelia and Edward!'

'And finally, Lisa and I would like you all to raise your
glasses to those who couldn't be with us today. To absent
friends!'

'Please raise your glasses to our friends Fabian and Gail, who
are in France due to family bereavement. Our thoughts are
with them. To Fabian and Gail!'

Do's and don'ts

- Do instruct the guests as to what to do. For example: 'Please raise your glasses with me...' Give them time to do so before you launch into the actual toast.
- Do tell guests exactly what the wording of the toast is to be, for example: 'To the bridesmaids'. Clarity is the key to a good toast.
- Do keep your toast focused.
- Do make your toast positive or funny.
- Do finish your toast with a flourish and leave them wanting more.
- Do, after the toast, sit when the guests sit down.

- Don't rush into a toast before your guests have had time to follow your instructions or it will end up confused and only half-heard.
- Don't make your toast too wordy – or guests won't be able to follow it.

- Don't forget, where appropriate, to include your partner in the toast if she isn't going to make a speech, for example 'My wife and I would like to say a special thank you to the bridesmaids...'

Index

About confetti.co.uk

Confetti.co.uk, founded in 1999, is the leading destination for brides- and grooms-to-be. Every month over 700,00 people visit www.confetti.co.uk to help them plan their weddings and special occasions. Here is a quick guide to our website

Weddings The wedding channel is packed full of advice and ideas to make your day more special and your planning less stressful. Our personalized planning tools will ensure you won't forget a thing.

Celebrations Checklists, advice and ideas for every party and celebration.

Fashion and beauty View hundreds of wedding, bridesmaid and party dresses and accessories. Get expert advice on how to look and feel good.

Travel Search for the most idyllic destinations for your honeymoon, wedding abroad or romantic breaks. Get fun ideas for hen and stag weekends.

Suppliers Thousands of suppliers to choose from including venues, gift lists companies, cake makers, florists and bridal retailers.

Café Talk to other brides and grooms and get ideas from our real life weddings section. Ask Aunt Betti, our agony aunt, for advice.

Shop All your wedding and party essentials in one place. The ranges include planning essentials, books and CDs, personalised stationery for weddings and celebrations, create your own trims, ribbons and papers, table decorations, party products including hen and stag, memories and gifts. If you'd like to do your shopping in person or view all the ranges before buying online, please visit the confetti stores.

Online

• Shop online 24 hours a day 7 days a week, use quick searches by department, product code or keyword, use the online order tracking facility and view brand new products as soon as they come out.

• Shop by phone on 0870 840 6060 Monday to Friday between 9 am and 5 pm.

• Shop by post by sending a completed order form to Confetti, Freepost NEA9292, Carr Lane, Low Moor, Bradford, BD12 0BR or fax on 01274 805 741.

By phone/freepost

Request your free copy of our catalogue online at www.confetti.co.uk or call 0870 840 6060

In store

London – 80 Tottenham Court Road, London, W1T 4TE

Leeds – The Light, The Headrow, Leeds, LS1 8TL

Birmingham – 43 Temple Street, Birmingham B2 5DP

Glasgow – 15–17 Queen Street, Glasgow, G1 3ED

Reading – 159 Friar Street, Reading, RG1 1HE

Executive Editor **Katy Denny**
Managing Editor **Clare Churly**
Executive Art Editor **Penny Stock**
Design **Cobalt id**
Production Manager **Ian Paton**